William Nickle

**Honey out of the rock**

A compilation of sacred songs and hymns for use in gospel meetings and other

religious services

William Nickle

**Honey out of the rock**
*A compilation of sacred songs and hymns for use in gospel meetings and other religious services*

ISBN/EAN: 9783337266486

Printed in Europe, USA, Canada, Australia, Japan

Cover: Foto ©Thomas Meinert / pixelio.de

More available books at **www.hansebooks.com**

# HONEY OUT OF THE ROCK

A COMPILATION OF

## Sacred Songs and Hymns

FOR USE IN

## GOSPEL MEETINGS AND
## OTHER RELIGIOUS SERVICES.

EDITORS

W. S. NICKLE AND GEO. J. MEYER.

PUBLISHED BY
MEYER & BROTHER
108 Washington St.
CHICAGO.

May be ordered of Booksellers and Music Dealers.

# ✳ PREFACE····

"*HONEY OUT OF THE ROCK*" contains the latest and best pieces to be found in any of the recent compilations, together with a large number of the most useful and popular songs familiar to the public, and many others that are entirely new.

Its pages are enriched with some of the best productions of such writers as

| | | |
|---|---|---|
| Wm. J. Kirkpatrick | Jno. R. Sweeney | W. A. Ogden |
| J. H. Tenney | E. A. Hoffman | A. J. Gorden |
| Mrs. J. F. Knapp | R. E. Hudson | T. C. O'Kane |
| Chas. H. Gabriel | C. E. Leslie | E. O. Excell |
| J. H. Fillmore | H. H. McGranahan | A. Beirly |
| E S. Lorenz | J. H. Weber | P. Bilhorn |
| J. S. Norris | E. S. Ufford | I. N. McHose |
| J. H. Hall | J. M. Whyte | Mrs. M. E. Wilson |
| Nellie E. Fawcett | F. S. Shepard | W. G. Cooper |
| A. J. Showalter | A. F. Myers | M. L. McPhail |
| Frank M. Davis | Joshua Gill | E. F. Miller |
| L. E. Jones | Geo. C. Hugg | I. H. Meredith |
| Grant C. Tullar | W. W. Bentley | Dr. Lowell Mason |
| Miss Emma E. Meyer | H. R. Palmer | J. E. Rankin |
| Walter A. Keller | J. H. Stockton and others. | |

We have added a selection of Standard Hymns, new and old, especially for use in devotional meetings.

We send forth this book of song with the hope that it may prove acceptable to the worshipers of the Master, and help in some slight degree to swell the anthem of praise that, in constantly increasing volume, ascends to HIS DEAR NAME.

*W. S. NICKLE.*
*GEO. J. MEYER*

# "HONEY OUT OF THE ROCK."

**No. 1.**      Honey out of the Rock.

L. W. S.

LANTA WILSON SMITH.

1. Out in the des - ert of sin Je - sus found me, Lost in the depths of a
2. Now from the rich - es of grace He's be - stow- ing Won-der - ful bless-ings my
3. No one can tell all the joy of re -demption, No one describe half the
4. Come, sin-ner, come, there's a wide in - vi - ta - tion, Come with your sin-burdened,

sin-ner's de- spair, Gen - tly thro' paths of for - give- ness He led me,
joy to com-plete; Feed - ing my soul ev - 'ry day with His boun-ty—
bless-ings in store, No one can meas-ure the bliss of pos -sess - ing
hun - ger - ing heart, Think of the joy that is prom-ised the faith-ful—

**CHORUS.**

Spread-ing a feast in the wil - der - ness rare.
Hon - ey, and milk, and the best of the wheat. With hon -ey from the rock He is
Knowl-edge of par-don, and peace ev - er-more.
In all this bless-ed -ness you have a part.

feed-ing His peo - ple. Hon-ey from the rock, hon -ey from the rock, With

hon-ey from the rock He is feeding His peo-ple. Sweet are the gifts of God.

# No. 2.     Heaven is not Far Away.

C. E. L.

C. E. LESLIE. By per.

1. Heav - en is not far a - way, When Je - sus is near;
2. Will you not re - pent, be - lieve, When Je - sus is near?
3. Are you com - ing home to - day, When Je - sus is near?

Give your heart to Him, I pray, When Je - sus is near.
Peace and par - don now re - ceive, When Je - sus is near.
Do not long - er stay a - way, When Je - sus is near.

Place your trust in Him, dear friend, He will keep you to the end,
He will not your pray'r re - fuse, Come and now the Sav - ior choose,
Cast your bur - den on the Lord, He has prom - ised in His word,

*Rit.* . . . . . . . .

Heav - en is not far a - way, When Je - sus is near.
Heav - en is not far a - way, When Je - sus is near.
Heav - en is not far a - way, When Je - sus is near.

# No. 3. Toiling for Jesus.

W. A. O.

W. A. OGDEN.

*Spirited.*

1. Glad-ly, glad-ly toil-ing for the Mas-ter, Go we forth with
2. Sweet-ly, sweet-ly we will tell the sto-ry Of His love to
3. Meek-ly, meek-ly toil-ing for the Mas-ter, Walk-ing, faith-ful-

will-ing hands to do, What-so-e'er to us He hath ap-point-ed,
mor-tals here be-low; Christ, the brightness of the Fa-ther's glo-ry,
ly the path He trod; Lead-ing wand'rers to the dear Re-deem-er,

**CHORUS.**

Faith-ful-ly our mis-sion we'll pur-sue. Toil - - ing for
Free - ly here His bless-ing will be-stow. Toil-ing, toil-ing
Point-ing sin - ners to the Lamb of God.

Je - sus, Joy-ful-ly we go, yes, joy-ful-ly we go;
for the Mas-ter,

Toil - - ing for Je - sus, In His vine-yard here be - low.
Toil-ing, toil-ing for the Mas-ter,

# No. 4.  When Jesus Came My Way.

Rev. J. Hoffman Batten.                                  I. H. Meredith.

1. The beg - gar sat blind by the way-side road, Till Je - sus came a - long,
2. One word from the Mas - ter, his eyes gave sight, When Je - sus came a - long,
3. I heard the sweet sound of the an-gel throng, When Je - sus came a - long,
4. Oh! come to the Sav - ior; be heal'd of sin, To - day He comes a - long,

came a - long that way; And then he re-joic'd in the pow'r of God, When
came a - long that way; And faith in His word fill'd his heart with light, When
came a - long my way; As they join'd in the glad re-demp-tion song, When
comes a - long your way; The sin - ner, crys out, and the light breaks in, When

**Chorus.**

Je - sus came a - long that way.
Je - sus came a - long that way.
Je - sus came a - long my way.
Je - sus comes a - long that way.

My life was all dark - ened by
now 'tis all bright-ness and

guilt and sin, Till Je - sus came a - long, came a -
peace with - in, [ Omit . . . . . . . . . . .

long my way; But ]  Since Je - sus came a - long my way.

## No. 5.    The Very Same Jesus.

"This same Jesus."—Acts 1: 11.

L. H. Edmunds.          Wm. J. Kirkpatrick.

1. Come, sin - ners, to the Liv - ing One, He's just the same Je - sus
2. Come, feast up - on the "liv - ing bread," He's just the same Je - sus
3. Come, tell Him all your griefs and fears, He's just the same Je - sus
4. Come un - to Him for clear - er light, He's just the same Je - sus

As when He raised the wid - ow's son, The ver - y same Je - sus.
As when the mul - ti - tudes He fed, The ver - y same Je - sus.
As when He shed those lov - ing tears, The ver - y same Je - sus.
As when He gave the blind their sight, The ver - y same Je - sus.

CHORUS.

The ver - y same Je - sus, The won - der work - ing Je - sus;

Oh, praise His name, He's just the same, The ver - y same Je - sus.

5 Calm 'midst the waves of trouble be,
   He's just the same Jesus
As when He hushed the raging sea,
   The very same Jesus.

6 Some day our raptured eyes shall see
   He's just the same Jesus;
Oh, blessed day for you and me!
   The very same Jesus.

## No. 6. Marching on the Way.

Rev. H. G. Jackson, D. D.

*Spirited.*

Miss Emma E. Meyer.

1. We are marching on the way to the heav'n-ly land, With the ban-ner of our
2. We are marching on the way to the heav'n-ly land; All the journey thro' our
3. We are marching on the way to the heav'n-ly land, To the land of rest and

Cap-tain wav-ing o'er us, With the shield of faith and prayer, and with
Cap-tain safe-ly leads us, Lo! a fount-ain from the rock flows at
peace be-yond the riv-er; Soon we'll cross the mys-tic flood to the

sword in hand, All the hosts of sin and Sa-tan fly be-fore us.
His com-mand; And with man-na from the skies He dai-ly feeds us.
gold-en strand, There to sing and shout our Cap-tain's praise for-ev-er.

**CHORUS.**

We are march-ing on the way, We are march-ing on the way,

March-ing on the way to the heav'n-ly land; To the heav'n-ly land, A

# Marching on the Way. Concluded.

hap-py, hap-py band, We are marching on the way to the heav'n-ly land.

No. 7.
F. S. S.

# Harvest Fields.

John 4: 35.

F. S. SHEPARD.

1. See the shin-ing fields of wav-ing grain, See the har-vest-fields so white!
2. Hear the Sav-ior, as He call-eth thee To the har-vest-fields so white!
3. Haste! the Master's ur-gent call o-bey, See the har-vest-fields so white!

O - ver-spread-ing ev - 'ry hill and plain, See the har-vest-fields so white!
"Come and la - bor earn-est - ly for me In the har-vest-fields so white "
Quick-ly join the reap-er's ranks to - day In the har-vest-fields so white.

CHORUS.
There is work......that each may do,......Work for me........ and work for

There is work         each may do,         Work for me,

you.........

work for you, And the lab'rers are so ver-y few In the har-vest-field so white.

# No. 8. We're on the way to Canaan's Land.

Rev. H. G. Jackson.                                                        W. S. Nickle.

1. From E - gypt's cru - el bond - age fled, O - be - dient to our
2. Thro' wil - der - ness - es wide and drear, Our Lord will guide our
3. His pow'r the smit - ten rock con - trols, A crys - tal stream our
4. In hos - tile lands we feel no fear; No foe our on - ward
5. Ere long, the riv - er cross'd, we'll meet The ran - som'd host at

Lord's com - mand, And by His word and spir - it led, We're
steps a - right, Be - hold! to prove His pres - ence here, The
need sup - plies, He feeds our hun - gry, faint - ing souls, With
march can stay; In ev - 'ry con - flict He is near, Whose
His right hand; And there re - ceive a wel - come sweet, From

**Chorus.**

on the way to Ca - naan's land!
cloud by day, the fire by night!
dai - ly man - na from the skies!    We're on the way, a
pres - ence cheers us on the way.
our dear Lord to Ca - naan's land!

pil - grim land; We're on the way to Ca - naan's land; Di-

vine - ly guid - ed day by day, We're on the way, we're on the way.

# No. 9.    Beneath the Cross.

T. G. COLFAX.

GRANT C. TULLAR.

*With Vigor.*

1. Be - neath the cross of Je - sus My soul bowed down with sin;
2. Be - neath the cross of Je - sus My sins were washed a - way;
3. Be - neath the cross of Je - sus There's heal - ing now for thee;

'Twas there the Sav - ior found me, And there He took me in.
My gar - ments died in crim - son, Were changed to white ar - ray.
The Sav - ior longs, in mer - cy, To cleanse and set you free.

Be - neath the cross, the bless - ed cross, Where Je - sus bled and died,
There 'neath the cross, the bless - ed cross, I found the heal - ing balm;
'Twas at the cross the Sav - ior paid Your ran - som from the fall;

My soul has found a ref - uge sweet, And there will I a - bide.
For ev - 'ry woe and ill of life, In tem - pest or in calm.
So cast your tro - phies at His feet And crown Him Lord of all.

# No. 10.   Are You Walking in the Light?

Rev. J. H. W.                                                   Rev. J. H. WEBER.

1. Are you walk-ing in the light of the Sav - ior? Does the way seem bright and
2. Are you walk-ing in the light of the Sav - ior? Does His blood cleanse you from
3. Are you walk-ing in the light of the Sav - ior? Are you glad you have this

fair? Are you try - ing ev - 'ry day now to please Him? Do you hope to
sin? Are you liv - ing ev - 'ry day for His glo - ry? Is your life pure
light? Will you trust and o - bey and al - ways love Him? If He'll keep thy

CHORUS.

meet Him o-ver there? Are you walking in the light? Are your garments clean and white?
and spotless with-in?
soul so pure and white?

Are you trust-ing Him in ev - 'ry care? Are you walk-ing in the light?

Are your garments clean and white? Are you walking, walk-ing in the light?

# No. 11.     The Good Shepherd.

W. S. NICKLE.

1. Sav - ior, like a shep-herd lead us, Much we need Thy tend - rest care,
2. We are Thine, do Thou be-friend us, Be the Guard-ian of our way;
3. Thou hast prom-ised to re - ceive us, Poor and sin - ful though we be;
4. Ear - ly let us seek Thy fa - vor, Ear - ly let us do Thy will;

In Thy pleas - ant pas-tures feed us, For our use Thy folds pre - pare;
Keep Thy flock, from sin de - fend us, Seek us when we go a - stray;
Thou hast mer - cy to re - lieve us, Grace to cleanse, and pow'r to free;
Bless - ed Lord, and on - ly Sav-ior, With Thy love our bos - oms fill.

**Chorus.**

Lead us, lead us, Lead us with Thy ten - der care;

Lead us, lead us, For Thy use our souls pre - pare.

# Happy in Jesus.

FANNY J. CROSBY.　　　　　　　　　　　　　　WM. J. KIRKPATRICK.

1. Hap-py in　Je-sus, hap-py in　Je-sus, I will de-clare it　a - broad;
2. Clinging to　Je-sus, on - ly to　Je-sus, O what a com-fort　is mine;
3. Walking with Je-sus, on - ly with Je-sus, Sweet-ly I jour-ney　a - long;

Cho.—Hap-py in　Je-sus, hap-py in　Je-sus, I will de - clare it　a - broad.

FINE.

Thro' His a - tonement, precious a - tonement, I have found fa - vor with God.
I will a - dore Him, yes, I will praise Him, Je-sus, my Sav - ior di - vine.
I have believ'd Him, I have re-ceiv'd Him, He is my joy and my song.

Thro' His a - tonement, precious a - tonement, I have found fa-vor with God.

Kindly he sought me, ten-der-ly brought me Out of the des-ert so wild;
Under His watch-care peace-ful-ly hid - ing, Faith my Re - deemer can see;
Watching me ev - er, leaving me nev - er, Still my pro-tect - or is nigh;

D. C.

Now I can trust Him, thankfully trust Him, Since He has made me His child....
Angels in glo - ry, telling the sto - ry, Now are re - joic-ing with me....
Saved by His mer-cy, in - fi - nite mer-cy, Who is so hap - py as　I?....

# No. 13. They Crucified Him.

J. M. W.

J. M. WHYTE.

1. Come, sin - ner, be - hold what Je - sus hath done,
2. From heav - en He came, He loved you— He died;
3. No pit - y - ing eye, a sav - ing arm, none,
4. They cru - ci - fied Him, and yet He for - gave,
5. So what will you do with Je - sus your King?

Be - hold how He suf - fered for thee: They cru - ci - fied Him,
Such love as His nev - er was known; Be - hold! on the cross
He saw us and pit - ied us then; A - lone in the fight,
"My Fa - ther, for - give them," He cried; What must He have borne,
Say, how will you meet Him at last? What plea in the day

God's in - no - cent Son, For - sak - en, He died on the tree!
your King cru - ci - fied, To make you an heir to His throne!
the vic - t'ry He won; Oh, praise Him, ye chil - dren of men.
the sin - ner to save, When un - der the bur - den He died!
of wrath will you bring, When of - fers of mer - cy are past!

**CHORUS.**

They cru - ci - fied Him, they cru-ci-fied Him, They nailed Him to the tree,

And so there He died, A King cru - ci - fied, To save a poor sin - ner like me.

like me.

# No. 14. Throw Open the Gates.

L. E. Jones.  Isa 26; 2.  W. S. Nickle.

1. Throw o - pen the gates of the cit - y, The cit - y of
2. Throw o - pen the gates of the cit - y, The cit - y of
3. Throw o - pen the gates of the cit - y, Let it's glo - ry shine

crys - tal and gold, That all who ac - cept of the Sav - ior May
joy and of love, That its light may shine out on the pathway That
out like a star, That the mil - lions who know not the Sav - ior May

en - ter with joy to the fold.
leads to bright mansions a - bove.
hast - en from near and a - far.

**CHORUS.**

Throw o - pen the gates of the cit - y, That its light may shine out on the way; Throw o - pen the gates of the cit - y, We are near - ing its por - tals to - day.

## No. 15     They're All Taken Away.

Rev. J. H. Weber.

Arr. by Rev. J. H. Weber.

1. I came to Je - sus as I was, He took my sins a - way;
2. The blood of Christ will make you white, And wash your sins a - way;
3. Oh do con - fess your sins to him, He'll take them all a - way,

I put them all on Je sus Christ, And now they're tak-en a - way.
Oh, come and take Him as your Lord, He'll cleanse your guilt, all a - way.
And then you'll shout and sing His praise, Be-cause they're tak en a - way.

**CHORUS.**

They're all tak - en a - way (a-way), They're all tak - en a - way (a-way),

They're all tak - en a - way, ...... Thro' the blood ..... of the Lamb.
a - way,     the blood

2

# No. 16. Trusting Jesus Every Hour.

Dedicated to Miss Hattie Hopkins.

BENJ. HOPKINS.                                                NELLIE E. FAWCETT.

1. I am the Lord's and He is mine, He fills me with His love di - vine,
2. I've given my - self to Him a - lone, Not for one fault can I a - tone;
3. I'm serv - ing Him with my whole heart, From my dear Sav-ior I'll not part;
4. Lord, let me serve Thee with my might, Trust all to Thee and do the right;

He saved me by His grace and power, Now I am trusting ev - 'ry hour.
The blood of Christ was shed for me, From sin to cleanse and set me free.
His lov - ing arms 'round me en-twine, And not one friend so true I find.
Thy pre-cious life that Thou hast given, Has paved the passage - way to heaven.

CHORUS.

Trusting, trusting, trusting, trusting, I am trusting Je - sus ev - 'ry hour;

Trusting, trusting, trusting, trusting, I am trusting Je - sus ev - 'ry hour.

# No. 17. Jesus Will Bear Me O'er.

L. E. JONES.

W. S. NICKLE.

1. When I have reached earth's bor-der - land, Je - sus will bear me a - way;
2. Cit - y of glo-ry so bright and fair, Cit - y of peace a - bove.
3. Dwelling with Jesus in glo - ry - land, What could I ask be - side?

Take me to sing with the ransomed band, Hap-py in end - less day.
I shall sing prais - es to Je - sus there, Tell-ing His won-drous love.
Sing-ing the song of the an - gel - band, Near to the Sav - ior's side.

**CHORUS.**

Car - ried a - way to the realms of light, Safe on the gold - en shore;

In - to the sum - mer-land ev - er bright Je - sus will bear me o'er.

# No. 18.    There is Glory in my Soul.

Mrs. Grace Weiser Davis.          Chas. H. Gabriel.

1. Since I lost my sins, and I found my Sav-ior, There is glo-ry
2. Since He cleansed my heart and gave love's blest full-ness, There is glo-ry
3. Since I walk with God hav-ing sweet com-mun-ion, There is glo-ry
4. I have en-ter'd Canaan on my way to heav-en, There is glo-ry

in my soul! Since I lost my bur-den and found God's fa-vor, There is
in my soul! Since He keeps me ful-ly in lov-ing kindness, There is
in my soul! Bright-er grows each day in this heav'nly union,—There is
in my soul! And I claim as mine all my God has giv-en, There is

CHORUS.

glo-ry in my soul. Yes, there's glo-ry, glo-ry, there is glo-ry in my soul!

Ev-'ry day bright-er grows, And I con-quer all my foes; There is glo-ry,

glo-ry, yes, there's glo-ry in my soul, There is glo-ry in my soul!

# No. 19.  I Have Found It!

ABBIE MILLS.  W. S. NICKLE.

1. I have found the o-pened fount-ain, I have plunged be-neath the blood,
2. Rest in Je - sus, I have found it! Oh, the sweet, the heav'n-ly calm,
3. Oh, that day! I'll ne'er for - get it! When the Ho - ly Ghost came in,
4. Now His eas - y yoke I'm wear-ing, And He makes my joy com-plete,
5. Oh, to tell the world, I'm long - ing Of this o - pen, cleans-ing tide,

Flow-ing from the wounds of Je - sus, Pre-cious, crim-son, crys - tal flood.
That is brood - ing o'er my spir - it Since I knew the fount-ain's balm.
To my heart the blood re - veal - ing, That has cleans'd me from all sin.
While I'm learn-ing bless - ed les - sons, Where He guides my will - ing feet.
That will wash and make all read - y For a place at Je - sus' side.

CHORUS.

I have found it! I have found it! Found the crys - tal, heal-ing flood;

Hal - le - lu - jah! for my cleans-ing, There is pow'r in Je - sus' blood!

# No. 20. Will the Gates of Heaven be Open to Me?

E. R. Latta.

C. E. Leslie. By per.

1. When my work is fin - ish'd, I'm try - ing to do, For my
2. When my toil - some jour - ney is end - ed be - low, And my
3. When the tears of sor - row, so com - mon to all, And my
4. Where no death nor sick - ness can ev - er - more come, And the

dear Re - deem - er, tho' hum - ble I be; Will the gold - en cit - y a -
feet, so wea - ry, for - ev - er are free, Will the walls of jas - per ef -
scene of trou - ble com - plet - ed shall be, Will the voice of Je - sus in
loved, if ho - ly, each oth - er shall see, Will I there be wel - comed, no

rise to my view?
ful - gent - ly flow?  } Will the gates of heav - en be o - pen to me?
ten - der - ness call?
long - er to roam?

**CHORUS.**

O - pen to me, O - pen to me, Will the gates of heaven be o - pen to me, Will the

gold - en cit - y a - rise to my view, Will the gates of heaven be o - pen to me?

# No. 21. Just Beyond the River.

FRED WOODROW.  T. C. O'KANE.

1. There's a cit - y bright and fair, Just be-yond, be - yond the riv - er,
2. Sin and sor - row are no more, Just be-yond, be - yond the riv - er,
3. There we shall with Je - sus meet, Just be-yond, be - yond the riv - er,
4. In that cit - y bright and fair, Just be-yond, be - yond the riv - er,

All are good and hap - py there, Just be-yond, be - yond the riv - er:
Death comes not up - on the shore, Just be-yond, be - yond the riv - er;
And the good in glo - ry greet, Just be-yond, be - yond the riv - er;
All at last may gath - er there, Just be-yond, be - yond the riv - er;

Streets of gold are shin - ing bright, An - gels walk the plains of light,
None are sad with want or care, Pain or sick - ness none shall bear,
Lives whose tale no tongue has told, Men of God and saints of old,
We may meet to part no more,—All our troub - les will be o'er,

**FINE.**

And there nev - er com - eth night, Just be - yond, be - yond the riv - er.
All are hap - py "o - ver there," Just be - yond, be - yond the riv - er.
Mar-tyrs with their crowns of gold, Just be - yond, be - yond the riv - er.
When we reach that "shin-ing shore," Just be - yond, be - yond the riv - er.

**REFRAIN.**  **D. S.**

Just be - yond....... the riv - er, Just be - yond ...... the riv - er.
Just be-yond the riv - er. Just be-yond the riv - er.

# No. 22. Wonderful Bible.

Rev. H. G. Jackson. D. D.

Miss Emma E. Meyer

1. Won-der - ful Bi - ble! Book of God; Guide and coun - sel to
2. Won-der - ful Bi - ble! Law of the Lord; All its pre-cepts in
3. Won-der - ful Bi - ble! Ra - diance bright; Ray se - rene from the

mor - tals giv'n; Lamp to the path by the ran - somed trod,
grace a - bound; And in their keep - ing is great re - ward,
world a - bove, Fair - est of stars in hu - man-i - ty's night,

CHORUS.

Light-ing the way from earth to heav'n. )
Life ev - er - last - ing there is found. } Shine, O won-der - ful
Fill now our hearts with light and love. )

light di - vine, Lamp of Truth, in this dark world shine, Shine thro' the

night of doubts and fears, Shine till the morn of God ap - pears!

# No. 23.   I Always Go to Jesus.

G. W. FIELDS.

1. "I al - ways go to Je - sus" When troub-led or dis - tressed;
2. When full of dread fore - bod - ings, And flow - ing o'er with tears,
3. "I al - ways go to Je - sus!" No mat - ter when or where

I al - way find a ref - uge Up - on His lov - ing breast.
He calms a - way my sor - row, And hush - es all my fears.
I seek His gra - cious pres - ence, I'm sure to find Him there.

I tell Him all my tri - als, I tell Him all my grief;
He com - pre - hends my weak-ness, The per - il I am in,
In times of joy or sor - row, What-e'er my need may be,

And while my lips are speak - ing, He gives my heart re - lief.
And He sup - plies the ar - mor I need to con - quer sin.
I al - ways go to Je - sus, And Je - sus comes to me.

# No. 24     Glorious Fountain.

COWPER.

T. C. O'KANE. By per.

1. There is a fountain filled with blood, filled with blood, filled with blood,
2. The dy-ing thief re-joiced to see, rejoiced to see, re-joiced to see,
3. Thou dy-ing Lamb, Thy precious blood, Thy precious blood, Thy precious blood,
4. E'er since by faith I saw the stream, I saw the stream, I saw the stream,

There is a fountain filled with blood, Drawn from Immanuel's veins, And
The dy - ing thief re-joiced to see That fountain in his day; And
Dear dy - ing Lamb! Thy precious blood Shall nev - er lose its power, Till
E'er since by faith, I saw the stream Thy flowing wounds sup - ply, Re-

sinners plunged beneath that flood, beneath that flood, beneath that flood, And
there may I though vile as he, though vile as he, though vile as he, And
all the ransomed Church of God, Church of God, Church of God, Till
deeming love has been my theme, has been my theme, has been my theme, Re-

CHORUS.

sinners plunged beneath that flood, Lose all their guilty stains. ⎤
there may I, tho' vile as he, Wash all my sins a - way. ⎟  Oh, glo-ri-ous
all the ransomed Church of God Are saved to sin no more. ⎟
deeming love has been my theme, And shall be till I die. ⎦

fountain! Here will I stay, And in Thee ev - er Wash my sins a - way.

Copyright, 1881, by T. C. O'Kane.

## No. 25. Come away to Jesus Now.

J. M. W.

J. M. Whyte.

1. Oh, why thus stand with re - luc - tant feet, Just on the verge
2. The Spir - it strives, and yet there you stand, In sight of bliss
3. Your loved ones gone to the oth - er shore, With un - seen hands
4. The touch of death is up - on your frame, The mar - ble slab

of this rest so sweet? While God in - vites and your steps will greet,
and the glo - ry land; Re - treat is death in the sink - ing sand,
seem to beck - on o'er; Their voic - es hushed, yet they still im - plore,
soon will bear your name; Lest you should suf - fer e - ter - nal shame,

**CHORUS.**

Come a - way to Je - sus now. Come a - way to Je - sus, Come a -
Come a - way to Je - sus, come a - way,

way to Je - sus, Come a - way to
Come a - way to Je - sus, come a - way, Come a - way to

Je - sus, Come a - way to Je - sus now.
Je - sus, come a - way,

# No. 26.     The Pilgrim Way.

Rev. H. G. Jackson, D. D.

Miss Emma E. Meyer.

1. Up-ward toils the ea - ger pil-grim, Press-ing on - ward to his home,
2. Oft the way is rough and thorn - y, And the pil - grim's feet are bare,
3. Oft he jour - neys thro' the val - ley, And the night seems dark and long,
4. Sometimes too, from mount or hill - top, His en - rapt - ured eyes be - hold,
5. Soon he'll cross the mys - tic riv - er, And on yon - der peace-ful shore,

Now in sun-shine, now in shad-ow—But the per-fect day will come.
But his Lord hath once passed o'er it, Leav-ing shin-ing foot-prints there.
But the joy that comes with morning, Turns his sor - row in - to song.
Gleaming in the sun - set glo - ry, Gates of pearl and streets of gold!
All his wea - ry wand'rings end - ed, Dwell with Je - sus ev - er - more.

CHORUS.

Yes, the path - way grow-eth bright-er, Grow-eth bright - er all the way,

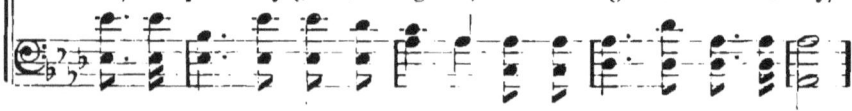

As it nears the heav'nly cit - y, And the realms of end - less day.

# No. 27. Jesus will Carry Me Over the River.

Yea, though I walk through the valley of the shadow of death, I will fear no evil, for thou art with me. Ps. 23: 4.     Words and Music by A. F. MYERS.

**Slow.**

1. I know, at the riv-er of death, My Sav-ior will be at my
2. I fear not to en-ter the flood, Tho' wild-ly its bil-lows may
3. I know when the riv-er I cross That Je-sus will car-ry me
4. Oh, when to cross o-ver the tide, To me the glad summons shall

side; His pres-ence so near Will ban-ish all fear, And
roll, With Je-sus my guide, No ill can be-tide, For
o'er; Up-held by His arm, I'll suf-fer no harm, But
come, With Christ as my light, The way will be bright, And

**CHORUS.**

He will the wa-ters di-vide.
He will the tem-pest con-trol.
safe-ly I'll reach the blest shore.
an-gels will wel-come me home.

Yes, Je-sus will car-ry me

o-ver the riv-er, Yes, Je-sus will car-ry me o'er, (yes, o'er:) He'll

**Rit.**

car-ry me o'er to the glo-ri-fied shore, Yes, Je-sus will car-ry me o'er.

# No. 28. Wilt Thou be Made Whole?

W. J. K.

Wm. J. Kirkpatrick. By per.

1. Hear the foot-steps of Je - sus, He is now pass-ing by, Bear-ing balm for the
2. 'Tis the voice of that Sav - ior Whose mer-ci - ful call Free-ly of - fers sal-
3. Are you halt-ing and struggling, O'erpow'rd by your sin, While the waters are
4. Bless - ed Sav-ior, as - sist us To rest on Thy word; Let the soul healing

wounded, Heal-ing all who ap - ply; As He spake to the suff - 'rer Who
va - tion To one and to all; He is now beck'ning to Him Each
troub-led, Can you not en - ter in? Lo, the Sav - ior stands wait-ing To
pow - er On us now be out-pour'd: Wash a - way ev - ery sin - spot, Take

lay at the pool, He is say - ing this mo-ment, "Wilt thou be made whole?"
sin - taint-ed soul, And lov - ing - ly ask - ing, "Wilt thou be made whole?"
strengthen your soul, He is earn-est - ly plead-ing, "Wilt thou be made whole?"
per - fect con-trol, Say to each trust-ing spir - it, "Wilt thou be made whole?"

REFRAIN.

Wilt thou be made whole? Wilt thou be made whole? Oh, come, wea-ry

## Wilt Thou be Made Whole? Concluded.

suf-f'rer, Oh, come, sin-sick soul; See, the life-stream is flowing, See, the

cleansing waves roll: Step in - to the cur-rent and thou shalt be whole.

## No. 29.    Full Consecration.

JOSEPH STURMAN.                                    W. S. NICKLE.

1. Lord, for to - mor - row and its needs, I do not pray;
2. Let me both dil - i - gent - ly work, And du - ly pray;
3. Let me be slow to do my will, Prompt to o - bey;
4. Let me no wrong-ful, i - dle word, Un - thought - ful say;

Keep me, dear Friend, from stain and sin, Just for to - day.
Let me be Thine in word and deed, Just for to - day.
Help me, dear Lord, to sac - ri - fice, Just for to - day.
But keep me, guide me, hold me, Lord, Just for to - day.

# No. 30.  More about Jesus.

E. E. Hewitt.  JNO. R. SWENEY.

1. More a-bout Je - sus would I know, More of His grace to oth - ers show;
2. More a-bout Je - sus let me learn. More of His ho - ly will dis-cern;
3. More a-bout Je - sus; in His word, Hold-ing com-mun-ion with my Lord;
4. More a-bout Je - sus; on His throne, Rich-es in glo - ry all His own;

More of His sav - ing full-ness see, More of His love who died for me.
Spir - it of God, my teach-er be, Show-ing the things of Christ to me.
Hear - ing His voice in ev - 'ry line, Mak-ing each faith-ful say - ing mine.
More of His kingdom's sure in-crease, More of His com-ing, Prince of Peace.

**REFRAIN.**

More, more a - bout Je - sus, More, more a - bout Je - sus;

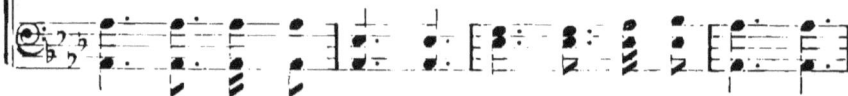

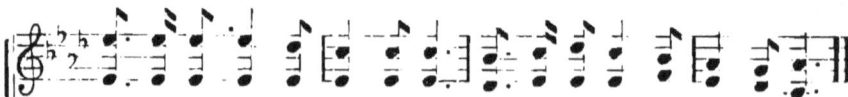

More of His sav - ing full-ness see, More of His love who died for me.

## No. 31. Wonderful Peace.

Rev. W. D. Cornell. Alt.

Rev. W. G. Cooper.

1. Far a-way in the depths of my spir-it to-night, Rolls a
2. What a treas-ure I have in this won-der-ful peace, Bur-ied
3. I am rest-ing to-night in this won-der-ful peace, Rest-ing
4. And me-thinks when I rise to that Cit-y of Peace, Where the
5. Ah! soul, are you here with-out com-fort or rest, March-ing

mel - o - dy sweet-er than psalm; In ce - les - tial-like strains it un-
deep in the heart of my soul; So deep that no pow - er can
sweet-ly in Je - sus' con - trol; For I'm kept from all dan - ger by
Au - thor of peace I shall see; That one strain of the song which the
down the rough pathway of time! Make Je - sus your friend ere the

ceas - ing-ly falls O'er my soul like an in - fi - nite calm.
mine it a - way, While the years of e - ter - ni - ty roll.
night and by day, And His sun - shine is flood - ing my soul.
ran-somed will sing, In that heav - en - ly king - dom will be,
shad - ows grow dark, Oh, ac - cept of this peace so sub - lime.

CHORUS.

Peace! peace! wonder-ful peace, Coming down from the Fa - ther a - bove; Sweep

o - ver my spir-it for - ev - er, I pray, In fath-om-less bil-lows of love.

# No. 32. Leaning on the Everlasting Arms.

Rev. E. A. Hoffman.   Deut. 33: 27.   A. J. Showalter.

1. What a fel-low-ship, what a joy di-vine, Lean-ing on the ev-er-
2. Oh, how sweet to walk in this pil-grim way, Lean-ing on the ev-er-
3. What have I to dread, what have I to fear, Lean-ing on the ev-er-

last-ing Arms. What a bless-ed-ness, what a peace is mine,
last-ing Arms, Oh, how bright the path grows from day to day,
last-ing Arms? I have bless-ed peace with my Lord so near,

CHORUS.

Lean-ing on the ev-er-last-ing Arms. Lean - - ing.
Lean-ing on Je-sus,

lean - ing, Safe and se-cure from all a-larms, Lean - ing,
lean-ing on Je-sus, Lean-ing on Je-sus,

lean - - - ing, Lean-ing on the ev-er-last-ing Arms.
lean-ing on Je-sus,

By per. of A. J. Showalter, Dalton, Ga.

# No. 33. Call to the Children.

Rev. H. Skeel.

W. S. Nickle.

1. Oh, sweet is the voice of my Sav - ior, With ac - cents of
2. He o - pens His arms to re - ceive them, With bless - ing and
3. Oh, list - en to Je - sus, your Sav - ior, His life for your
4. Oh, Spir - it, still strive with the chil - dren! Oh, Sav - ior, still

ten - der - est love; Now call - ing His dear lit - tle chil - dren To
par - don of sin; He wash - es a - way their trans - gres - sions, And
ran - som He gave; He calls you to come to His king - dom, To-
call them to Thee! O chil - dren, be - lieve now in Je - sus, For

**CHORUS.**

come to His man - sions a - bove.
wel - comes the lit - tle ones in.
day He is wait - ing to save.
you His sal - va - tion is free.

Oh, come while the Sav - ior is

call - ing, So ten - der - ly plead - ing—Oh, come! Be saved from your

sins, and for - ev - er A - bide in His heav - en - ly home.

# No. 34. Keep Moving on the Way.

E. S. U.  *Jubilee Melody.*  Rev. E. S. Ufford.

*Lively.*

1. There is on - ly one thing that the Christ - ian needs to do,
2. Oh, this se - cret of pro - gress - ing, ev - 'ry - bod - y ought to keep,
3. In the gal - ler - ies of the skies an - gel hosts are look - ing down,

As he jour - neys with the saints to end - less day; If he'd
For this earth - ly life will nev - er, nev - er pay, If we
And they watch us as we strug - gle day by day; To the

keep his soul from fall - ing while the way he does pur - sue, Is to
lay a - side the cross and re - sign our eyes to sleep, And for -
vic - tor in the race God will give a star - ry crown, If we

**CHORUS.**

ev - er keep moving on the way. Keep mov - ing on the way,
get to keep moving on the way.
ev - er keep moving on the way. Keep mov - ing on the way,

Let us ev - er keep mov - ing on the way, Keep mov - ing
on the way. Keep mov - ing

## Keep Moving on the Way. Concluded.

on the way;
on the way;
Let us ev - er keep mov - ing on the way.

## No. 35.        I'll Trust Him.

W. H. GARDNER.                                        J. H. TENNEY.

1 I'll trust Thee, bless-ed Lord, Al - tho' the shad-ows come: Suf - fi - cient is Thy
2. I'll trust Thee, Master dear, For Thou art ev - er nigh: Thou dri - est ev -'ry
3. I'll trust Thee, Je - sus mine, Thou art my on - ly guide: My hand I'll place in
4. I'll trust Thee, sin-less One, For Thou didst die for me; O Christ, the Father's

CHORUS.

word, .. Thou pure and ho-ly One! I'll trust...... Thee, oh, I'll trust      Thee,
tear, ... That gath-ers in my eye.
Thine:. Be-neath Thy wings I'll hide.
Son, .... My life I give to Thee!      I'll ev-er trust Thee,      I'll ever trust Thee:

Ev    -    er - more      I'll      trust Thee; I      know.........Thine arms are
Ev - er-more, yes, ev - er-more I'll trust Thee,      I know Thine arms,

Rit.

'round      me, Wher - ev - er      I      may be, .....Wher-ev - er      I      may be.
Thine arms are 'round me, Wherev-er

# No. 36.     The Voice of Jesus.

EDITH G. CHERRY.

M. L. McPHAIL.

1. I have heard Thy voice, Lord Je-sus, Say-ing, in Thy grace di-vine:
2. I have noth-ing worth Thy tak-ing, Thou whom high-est heav'ns a-dore!
3. All, yes, all for Thee, Lord Je-sus! Sealed and pur-chased by Thy blood;

"Fear thou not, I have re-deemed thee; I have called thee, thou art mine."
But my heart is long-ing, yearn-ing, To be Thine for-ev-er more;
Thine am I, Thou Son of Da-vid, Thine am I, Thou Son of God.

So I come to Thee, Lord Je-sus, So I yield Thee ev-'ry thing,
Long-ing but to own Thee Mas-ter, Yearn-ing, in o-be-dience meet,
All the heart-re-bell-ion end-ed, All the half-al-le-giance past,

CHO.—All for Je-sus! All for Je-sus! All for Him who died for me;

_D. S. Chorus._

Answ'ring, "Yea Thou hast re-deemed me; I am Thine, my King, my King!"
All I am, and have, and hope for, To sur-ren-der at Thy feet.
All Thy right-ful king-ship own-ing, I am Thine, at last, at last.

Ev-er, on-ly, all for Je-sus, Now and through e-ter-ni-ty!

# No. 37.     Jesus Only.

ELIAS MASON.
           E. M. HERNDON.

1. Je - sus on - ly, when the morning Beams up - on the path I tread;
2. Je - sus on - ly, when the bil - lows Cold and sul - len o'er us roll;
3. Je - sus on - ly, sing - ing, prais-ing, Saints their crowns be-fore Him bring,

Je - sus on - ly, when the dark-ness Gath-ers round my wea - ry head.
Je - sus on - ly, when the trump-et Rends the tomb and wakes the soul.
Je - sus on - ly, I will joy - ous, Thro' e - ter - nal a - ges sing.

**CHORUS.**

Je - sus on - ly, Je - sus on - ly, He is near me day by day;

Je - sus on - ly, Je - sus on - ly, He goes with me all the way.

# No. 38.     Grace Abounding.

ABBIE MILLS.           W. S. NICKLE.

1. Up! a - way! help tell the sto - ry Of this grace - a - bound-ing glo - ry,
2. Up! a - way! the time re-deem-ing; Noon-tide light e'en now is beaming,
3. Grace a - bound-ing, on-ward go - ing, Just for sin - ners o - ver - flow-ing;
4. All thro' grace are robes made whiter Than the snow; and crowns are brighter
5. Up! a - way! help tell the sto - ry Of this grace - a - bound-ing glo - ry,

Ransomed ones, with much for giv- en; Point the way to peace and heav-en.
They who long have slept, are waking, Na - tions from sin's thralldom breaking.
Woo - ing, cleans ing, ev - er healing, Love of heav'n to hearts re - veal-ing.
That are God's be- loved a - dorn-ing, Than the bright- est star of morning.
Soft - ly speak of Calv'ry's mountain, Shout be-side the cleans-ing fountain.

**CHORUS.**

Hal-le - lu - jah! grace - a bound ing, This the news thro' earth resounding,

*Rit.*

Christ be - stow-ing—glorious Giv-er—Grace is flow- ing—bless-ed riv -er!

# No. 39. I Will Trust in the Blood of the Lamb.

C. WESLEY.

T. C. O'KANE. By per.

1. For - ev - er here my rest shall be, Close to Thy bleed-ing side;
2. My dy - ing Sav - ior and my God,—Fountain for guilt and sin,
3. Wash me, and make me thus Thine own; Wash me, and mine Thou art;
4. The a - tone-ment of Thy blood ap - ply, Till faith to sight im - prove;

This all my hope and all my plea,—For me the Sav - ior died.
Sprink-le me ev - er with Thy blood, And cleanse, and keep me clean.
Wash me, but not my feet a - lone,—My hands, my head, my heart.
Till hope in full fru - i - tion die, And all my soul be love.

CHORUS.

I will trust, I will trust, I will trust in the blood of the Lamb; I will

trust,....... I will trust,.... .. I will trust in the blood of the Lamb.

# No. 40.     I've Found a Friend.

M. L. McPhail.

1. I've found a friend: oh! such a friend! He loved me ere I knew him;
2. I've found a friend: oh! such a friend! He gave His life to save me;
3. I've found a friend: oh! such a friend! So kind, and true, and ten-der;

He drew me with the cords of love, And thus He bound me to Him.
And not a-lone the gift of life, But His own self He gave me.
So wise a coun-sel-or and guide, So might-y a de-fend-er!

And round my heart still close-ly twine Those ties which none can sev-er,
Naught that I have my own I call, I hold it for the Giv-er;
From Him who now doth love me so, What pow'r my soul can sev-er?

For I am His and He is mine, For-ev-er and for-ev-er.
My heart, my strength, my life, my all, Are His, and His for-ev-er.
Shall life, or death, or an-y foe? No: I am His for-ev-er.

# No. 41.     Nearer the Cross.

Mrs. FANNY J. CROSBY.               Mrs. J. F. KNAPP.

1. "Near-er the cross!" my heart can say, I am com-ing near-er, Near-er the
2. Near-er the Christian's mer-cy seat, I am com-ing near-er, Feast-ing my
3. Near-er in pray'r my hope as-pires, I am com-ing near-er, Deep-er the

cross from day to day, I am com-ing near-er; Near-er the cross where
soul on man-na sweet, I am com-ing near-er; Stronger in faith, more
love my soul de-sires, I am com-ing near-er; Near-er the end of

Je-sus died, Near-er the fount-ain's crim-son tide, Near-er my Sav-ior's
clear I see Je-sus who gave Him-self for me; Near-er to Him I
toil and care, Near-er the joy I long to share, Near-er the crown I

wound-ed side, I am com-ing near-er, I am com-ing near-er.
still would be: Still I'm com-ing near-er, Still I'm com-ing near-er.
soon shall wear: I am com-ing near-er, I am com-ing near-er.

By permission.

# No. 42.     Jesus, Our Friend.

LANTA WILSON SMITH.                        Mrs. W. S. NICKLE.

1. When Je - sus lived up - on the earth, And healed the sick and lame;
2. Per - haps these lit - tle boys and girls Were sometimes naughty too;
3. When lit - tle chil - dren come to Him, He takes them in his arms;

The moth - ers took their lit - tle ones, And joy - ful - ly they came.
But Je - sus sent them not a - way, His love is strong and true.
Oh, what a safe and bless - ed place To rest from all a - larms.

He looked on them and kind - ly said: "O let them come to Me.
Al-though He grieves when we do wrong, And slight His pre - cious name,
And so we sing with hap - py hearts, Our songs of joy and love;

For - bid them not, for such as these My Fa - ther's face shall see."
He tries to help us all the more, And loves us just the same.
We'll serve our bless - ed Sav - ior here, And dwell with Him a - bove.

# Jesus, Our Friend. Concluded.

CHORUS.

Our Sav-ior blessed the lit-tle ones, That all the world may know,

*Rit.*

He came to save the chil-dren too, Be-cause He loved them so.

## No. 43. Are the Children all in?

O. E. M.　　　　　　　　　　　　　　　Rev. O. E. Murray, A. M., B. D.

1. Are the chil-dren all in? Faith-ful moth-ers oft-en say,
2. Are the chil-dren all in? Are they sheltered from the cold?
3. Are the chil-dren all in? Moth-er whispered at the last.
4. Are the chil-dren all in? Win them, par-ents, do not wait!

Cho. *Are the chil-dren all in? Are they safe from ev-'ry sin?*

**D. C. for Chorus.**

As the cur-tains of the night Close a-round the dy-ing day.
Je-sus wants the pre-cious lambs For His bless-ed up-per fold.
As her chil-dren gath-ered 'round, When to glo-ry-land she passed.
Bring the lambs to Je-sus now, Or it soon may be too late.

*Fa-ther! moth-er! how can you rest, Till each lit-tle one is in?*

# No. 44. When the Roll is Called up Yonder.

B. M. J.

J. M. BLACK

1. When the trump - et of the Lord shall sound, and time shall be no
2. On that bright and cloud - less morn - ing when the dead in Christ shall
3. Let us la - bor for the Mas - ter from the dawn till set - ting

more, And the morn-ing breaks, e - ter - nal, bright and fair; When the
rise, And the glo - ry of His res - ur - rec - tion share; When His
sun, Let us talk of all His won-drous love and care, Then when

saved of earth shall gath - er o - ver on the oth - er shore, And the
chos - en ones shall gath - er to their home be - yond the skies, And the
all of life is o - ver and our work on earth is done, And the

**CHORUS.**

roll is called up yon - der, I'll be there. When the roll........ .... is
roll is called up yon - der, I'll be there.
roll is called up yon - der, I'll be there. When the roll is

called up yon - der, When the roll.......... is called up
called up yon-der. I'll be there, When the roll is called up

# When the Roll is Called up Yonder. Concluded.

you - - - der, When the roll............ is called up
you - der, I'll be there,        When the roll is called up

yon - der, When the roll is called up you - der, I'll be there

## No. 45.  Dropping Pennies.

Mrs. Fidelia H. DeWitt.  Wm. J. Kirkpatrick.

1. Hear the pen- nies drop ping, List - en while they fall, Ev - 'ry one for
2. Drop-ping, drop-ping ev - er, From each lit - tle hand, 'Tis our gift to
3. Now, while we are lit - tle, Pen - nies are our store, But, when we are
4. Tho' we have not mon - ey, We can give Him love, He will own our

### Refrain.

Je - sus, He will get them all.
Je - sus, From His lit - tle band.  } Drop-ping, drop ping dropping dropping,
old - er, Lord, we'll give thee more.
off - 'ring, Smil - ing from a - bove.

Hear the pen-nies fall;  Ev - 'ry one for Je - sus, He will get them all.

# No. 46.   What a Glorious Redeemer!

H. G. JACKSON, D. D.                                    A. BEIRLY.

1. My Sav - ior left His throne on high, And came to earth for
2. Be - neath the heav - y cross low bent, Up Cal - v'ry's rug - ged
3. That all might know His power to save, He rose in tri - umph
4. Reign too, O bless - ed King di - vine, For - ev - er in this

me to die; What a glo - rious Re - deem - er! At mid-night in Geth-
steeps He went; What a glo - rious Re - deem - er! From sin and death to
from the grave; What a glo - rious Re - deem - er! And now His cru - el
heart of mine; What a glo - rious Re - deem - er! Thy sov'-reign right in

sem - a - ne, He drank the bit - ter cup for me. What a glo - rious Re-
set me free, There on the cross He died for me. What a glo - rious Re-
suff'rings o'er, He reigns in bliss for - ev - er more. What a glo - rious Re-
me I own; In life or death I'm Thine a - lone. What a glor - rious Re-

**CHORUS.**

deem - er! What a glo - rious Re - deem - er is Je - sus, my

Sav - ior, What a glo - rious Re-deem - er is Je - sus, my Lord!

# No. 47. I Want to be There.

Harriet E. Jones.      I. H. Meredith.

1. { In the home of song and beau-ty, Where the ma - ny man-sions are,
{ Where the ran-som'd tell the sto - ry Of the earth - ly toil and care;

2. { Where are seen the o - ver - com - ers, With the shin - ing palms they bear,
{ Where the an - thems of re - demp-tion Fill with mu - sic all the air,

3. { Where the crowns of life are giv - en, All be decked with jew - els rare,
{ Thro' the ev - er - roll - ing a - ges, Where the skies are al - ways fair,

Where at last the saved shall gath - er, Oh, I want to be there. /
Of the cross they bore with Je - sus; Oh, I want to be there. {
Giv-ing Je - sus all the glo - ry; Oh, I want to be there. /
Join-ing in the song of rap - ture: Oh, I want to be there. {
Gathered thro' the earth - ly jour - ney; Oh, I want to be there. /
Basking in the smile of Je - sus; Oh, I want to be there. {

## CHORUS.

Oh, I want to be there, Yes, I want to be there,

With my Lord and dear Re-deem - er; Oh, I want to be there.

# No. 48. Sweet Resting By and By.

ELISHA A. HOFFMAN.　　　　　　　　　　　　　　T. C. O'KANE. By per.

1. We'll lay our heav - y bur - den down, By and by, By and by;
2. We,ll sing with all the ransom'd there, By and by, By and by;
3. We'll be with Je - sus where He is, By and by, By and by;

Ex-change the cross for the gold - en crown, By and by.....
And swell our praise on the balm - y air, By and by.....
A home more bright - ly fair than this, By and by.....

**CHORUS.**

There'll be sweet rest-ing by and by, By and by, by and by,

Sweet,........ sweet........ rest - ing by and by.....
Oh, how sweet! Oh, how sweet!

# No. 49. The Savior Calls To-day.

Rev. H. G. Jackson, D. D.　　　　　　　　　　　　　　Miss Emma E. Meyer.

1. O sin - ner, hear the Sav - ior's voice, He calls you,—haste a - way;
2. From fol - ly, un - be - lief and sin, He calls you,—haste a - way;
3. From soul - dis - tract - ing doubts and fears, He calls you,—haste a - way;
4. To pur - est bliss to mor - tals given, He calls you,—haste a - way;

Come, make His law of love your choice; He calls you,—come to - day.
From foes with - out and foes with - in, He calls you,—come to - day
From sor - row's un - a - vail - ing tears, He calls you,—come to - day.
To peace, and hope, and joy, and heav'n, He calls you,—come to - day.

CHORUS.

Come, sin - ner, come to - day, Come to the bless - ed Sav - ior,

Make no de - lay, but haste a - way; He calls you,—come to - day!

# No. 50. Blessed Jesus, Keep Me White.

P. B.

P. BILHORN.

1. Bless-ed Je - sus, Thou art mine, All I have is whol-ly Thine;
2. I am safe with-in the fold, All my cares on Thee are roll'd;
3. Pre-cious Je - sus, day by day, Keep me in the ho - ly way;

Thou dost dwell with-in my heart, Make me clean in ev - 'ry part.
I en - joy the sweet-est rest, For I'm lean-ing on Thy breast.
Keep my mind in per - fect peace, Ev - 'ry day my faith in-crease.

**CHORUS.**

white,..........

Bless-ed Je - - - sus, keep me white, keep me white, Keep me
Bless-ed Je - sus, keep me white,

walk - - - ing,

walk-ing, Keep me walk-ing in the light,...... All I have........ is
Keep me walk-ing in the light, All I have

whol-ly Thine,.......... Bless-ed Je - - - sus, Thou art mine.
is whol-ly Thine, Bless-ed Je - sus,

## No. 51. The Cleansing Wave.

"And washed us from our sins in His own blood." Rev. 13: 5.

Mrs. Phœbe Palmer.                     Mrs. Jos. F. Knapp.

1. Oh, now I see the crim-son wave, The fount - ain deep and wide;
2. I rise to walk in heav'n's own light A - bove the world and sin;
3. A - maz - ing grace! 'tis heav'n be - low To know the blood's ap - plied;
4. Oh, trust His grace! and prove His pow'r In sin though deep - ly dyed,

Je - sus, my Lord, might - y to save, Points to His wound - ed side.
With heart made pure and garments white, And Christ en-throned with in.
And Je - sus, on - ly Je - sus know, My Je - sus cru - ci - fied.
The Lamb of God this ver - y hour, Will speak Thee jus - ti - fied.

**CHORUS.**

The cleans-ing stream I see! I see! I plunge, and oh, it cleans-eth me,

Oh, praise the Lord, it cleans-eth me, yes, cleans-eth me, yes, cleans-eth me.

By permission.

# No. 52.     Tell it to Jesus.

C. H. G.

CHAS. H. GABRIEL.

1. Tell it to Je - sus— all of thy sor - row, All of thy
2. Tell it to Je - sus, He is thy Sav - ior, Tell it, and
3. Tell it to Je - sus, He is a ref - uge, In - to His

cares what - e'er they be; Sure - ly and sweet - ly, He will de - liv - er,
His sal - va - tion see; Do not de - ny Him, do not de - fy Him,
arms for mer - cy flee; Tell it be - liev - ing, tell it re - ceiv - ing,

CHORUS.

He will sus-tain and com-fort thee. Tell it to Je - sus, tell it to
He will sus-tain and com-fort thee.
Grace to sus-tain and com-fort thee.    Tell it to Je-sus,

Je - - sus. Tell it to Je - - sus, He will hear, On - ly be-
Tell it to Je - sus, Tell it to Je - sus,

lieve Him, trust and re-ceive Him, He will sus-tain and com -fort thee.

Copyright, 1891 and 1893, by Geo. F. Rosche. By per.

# No. 53.     Blessed Assurance.

F. J. CROSBY.     "He is faithful that hath promised." Heb. 10: 23.     Mrs. Jos. F. KNAPP.

1. Bless-ed as-sur-ance, Je-sus is mine! Oh, what a fore-taste of
2. Per-fect sub-mis-sion, per-fect de-light, Vis-ions of rap-ture
3. Per-fect sub-mis-sion, all is at rest, I in my Sav-ior am

glo-ry di-vine! Heir of sal-va-tion, pur-chase of God, Born of His
burst on my sight, An-gels de-scending, bring from a-bove Ech-oes of
hap-py and blest, Watching and wait-ing, look-ing a-bove, Filled with His

CHORUS.

Spir-it, washed in His blood...
mer-cy, whis-pers of love.... This is my sto-ry, this is my
good-ness, lost in His love....

song, Prais-ing my Sav-ior all the day long; This is my

sto-ry, this is my song, Prais-ing my Sav-ior all the day long.

# No. 54.  A Shelter in the Time of Storm.

A. J. Showalter.

1. The Lord's our Rock, in Him we hide, A shel-ter in the time of storm;
2. A shade by day, de-fence by night, A shel-ter in the time of storm;
3. The rag-ing storms may round us beat, A shel-ter in the time of storm;
4. O Rock di-vine, O Ref-uge dear, A shel-ter in the time of storm;

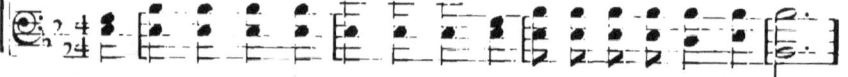

Se - cure what-ev - er may be - tide, A shel-ter in the time of storm.
No fears a - larm, no foes af-fright, A shel-ter in the time of storm.
We'll nev - er leave this safe re - treat, A shel-ter in the time of storm.
Be Thou our help - er ev - er near, A shel-ter in the time of storm.

**CHORUS.**

Oh, Je-sus is a rock in a wea-ry land, A wea-ry land, a wea-ry land;

Je-sus is a Rock in a wea-ry land, A shelter in the time of storm.

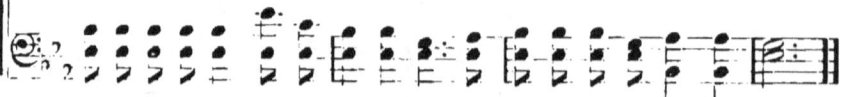

# No. 55. We Walk by Faith.

J. E. WOLFE.          P. BILHORN.

1. By child-like faith in Christ, the Lord, We have from sin sal - va - tion;
2. How sim - ple is the way of life, 'Tis on - ly to be - lieve Him;
3. Thro' Je - sus' death the debt was paid, Not feel - ing, nor e - mo - tion;
4. We walk by faith and not by sight, How grand is this re - veal - ing!

By ful - ly trust-ing in His word, We pass from con - dem - na - tion.
'Twill end your sor - row and your strife If you will but re - ceive Him.
On Him our sin and guilt was laid; O, give Him your de - vo - tion.
'Tis God's own way, and must be right, 'Tis wrong to trust in feel - ing.

**CHORUS.**

We walk by faith, and not by sight;
We walk by faith and not by sight; 'Tis God's own way and must be right;

We walk by faith,
We walk by faith and not by sight; We fol - low Christ, the Light.

# No. 56. The Blood of My Redeemer.

HENRIETTA E. BLAIR

WM. J. KIRKPATRICK.

1. I will praise the Lord for His love to me, I am wash'd in the blood of
2. I am saved by grace and to Him bro't near, I am wash'd in the blood of
3. What a con-stant peace in my heart I feel, I am wash'd in the blood of
4. I will lift my voice while on earth I stay, I am wash'd in the blood of

my Re-deem-er; In the fount that flows at the Cross so free, I am
my Re-deem-er; I would sing so loud that the world might hear, I am
my Re-deem-er; There's a ho-ly joy I can ne'er re-veal, I am
my Re-deem-er; Then my soul shall sing in the realms of day, I am

**REFRAIN.**

wash'd in the blood of my Re-deem-er.
wash'd in the blood of my Re-deem-er.
wash'd in the blood of my Re-deem-er.
wash'd in the blood of my Re-deem-er.

Glo-ry, glo-ry, glo-ry to the Lamb,

I am sav'd from sin and He makes me what I am; Oh, glo-ry, glo-ry,

glo-ry to the Lamb, I am wash'd in the blood of my Re-deem-er.

# No. 57. Lead Me, Savior.

F. M. D.

FRANK M. DAVIS.

*With expression.*

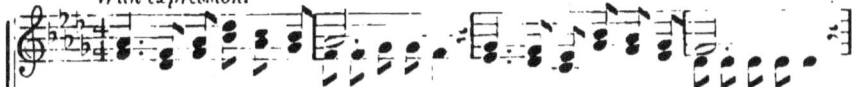

1. Sav-ior, lead me, lest I stray, Gen-tly lead me all the way:
2. Thou the refuge of my soul When life's stormy billows roll,
3. Sav-ior, lead me, then at last, When the storm of life is past,

1. Sav - ior, lead me, lest I stray, Gen - tly lead me all the way;

I am safe when by Thy side, I would in Thy love a-bide.
I am safe when Thou art nigh, All my hopes on Thee re-ly.
To the land of end-less day, Where all tears are wiped away.

I am safe when by Thy side, I would in Thy love abide.

### CHORUS.

Lead me, lead me, Sav - ior, lead me, lest I stray; .........
lest I stray;

*Rit. e dim.*

Gently down the stream of time, Lead me, Sav-ior, all the way.
stream of time, all the way.

From "Carols of Joy." By per.

# No. 58. Going Down the Valley.

JESSIE H. BROWN.　　　　　　　　　　　　　　　　　　J. H. FILLMORE.

1. We are go - ing down the val - ley, one by one, With our fac - es toward the
2. We are go - ing down the val - ley, one by one, When the la - bors of the
3. We are go - ing down the val - ley, one by one, Hu - man com-rade you or

set-ting of the sun; Down the val - ley where the mourn-ful cy - press grows,
wea-ry day are done; One by one, the cares of earth for - ev - er past,
I will there have none, But a ten - der Hand will guide us lest we fall.—

**CHORUS.**

Where the stream of death in si - lence on - ward flows. &#125;
We shall stand up - on the riv - er bank at last. &#125; We are go-ing down the
Christ is go - ing down the val - ley with us all. &#125;

val-ley, go - ing down the val-ley, Go-ing toward the setting of the sun, We are

going down the valley, go-ing down the valley, Going down the valley, one by one.

# No. 59. Where the Living Waters Flow.

Words arr.

EDWARD E. NICKERSON.

1. Rest to the wea-ry soul   And ach-ing breast is giv'n,   Down where the
2. For thee, my soul, for thee   These priceless joys were bought. Down where the
3. Come with the ransomed train,   The Sav-ior's prais-es sing,   Down where the
4. And soon, be-fore His face,   We'll praise in light a-bove,   Down where the

liv-ing wa-ters flow;   Grace makes the wounded whole, Love fills our heart with heav'n,
liv-ing wa-ters flow;   Thine is the mer-cy free, That Christ to earth has brought,
liv-ing wa-ters flow;   Re-joice! the Lamb was slain,   A-dore! He reigns a King,
liv-ing wa-ters flow;   Tri-umph-ant thro' His grace,   Made per-fect by His love,

### REFRAIN.

Down where the liv-ing wa-ters flow. Down where the living wa-ters flow,..........
living waters flow,

Down where the tree of life. doth grow,   I'm liv-ing in the light, for

Je-sus and the right,   Down where the liv-ing   wa-ters flow.
liv-ing wa-ters flow.

# No. 60. Come and See.

"Philip saith unto him, Come and see."

W. A. O.

W. A. OGDEN.

1. 'Tis the gos-pel in - vi - ta - tion, Come and see, come and see,
2. Oh, He nev - er will de - ceive you, Come and see, come and see,
3. Come to Je - sus now con - fid - ing, Come and see, come and see,

Un - to ev - 'ry tribe and na - tion, Come and see, come and see,
Of your bur - den He'll re - lieve you, Come and see, come and see,
In His shad - ow quick - ly hid - ing, Come and see, come and see,

Je - sus of - fers free sal - va - tion, come and see,
He is wait - ing to re - ceive you, come and see,
In His mer - cy there a - bid - ing, come and see, come and see,

What the Lord hath done for me.

CHORUS.

Come and see, come and see, come and see What the come and see, come and see

# Come and See.—Concluded.

Lord hath done for me, For He found my soul in sin, and He

washed me pure and clean. This the Lord hath done for me.

## No. 61.    Walk in the Light.

H. WATERS. Arr,

1. 'Tis re - li - gion that can give, In the light, in the light, Sweetest pleasures
2; 'Tis re - li - gion must sup-ply, In the light, in the light, Sol - id com-fort
3. Af - ter death its joys shall be, In the light, in the light, Last-ing as e -
4. Be the lov-ing God my friend, In the light, in the light, Then my bliss shall

while we live, In the light of God.
when we die, In the light of God.
ter - ni - ty, In the light of God.
nev - er end, In the light of God.

**CHORUS.**

Let us walk in the light,

Walk in the light, Let us walk in the light. In the light of God.

# No. 62.　　Draw Me Closer to Thee.

Mrs. E. W. Chapman.　　　　　　　　　　　　　　　　J. H. Tenney.

1. Clos - er to Thee, my Fa - ther, draw me, I long for Thine em-
2. Clos - er to Thee, my Sav - ior, draw me, Nor let me leave Thee
3. Clos - er by Thy sweet Spir - it draw me, Till I am whol - ly

brace; Clos - er with - in Thine arms en - fold me, I seek a rest - ing
more; Sigh - ing to feel Thine arms a - round me, And all my wand'rings
Thine; Quick-en, re - fine, and wash and cleanse me, Till pure my soul shall

CHORUS.

place. Clos - - - er with the cords of love,
o'er.
shine. Clos - er, clos - er with the cords of love,

Draw me to Thy-self a - bove; Clos - - - er
Draw me, draw me to Thy-self a - bove; Clos-er with the cords of love,

draw me To Thy - self a - bove.
Draw me to Thy - self a - bove, Draw me to Thy - self a - bove.

By permission.

# No. 63.    Crown Him.

IDA SCOTT TAYLOR.    GEO. F. ROSCHE.

1. Crown Him, crown Him, o - ver all na - tions vic - to - rious,
Crown Him, crown Him, tell of His king-dom all - glo - rious,
2. Crown Him, crown Him, now and for - ev - er a - dore Him,
Crown Him, crown Him, ye, who have wander'd, im - plore Him,

Shout ho - san - na! Je - sus has come to reign;
Raise the stand - ard, ev - er His cause main - tain.
Lo, He com - eth! glad - ly the news pro - claim;
Seek His par - don, He will your souls re - claim.

Laud Him! praise Him, join in the might-y cho - rus, Joy - ful sing the
Hail Him! bless Him, wor-ship and fall be - fore Him, Joy - ful sing the

### CHORUS.

song with its glad re - frain.
song with its glad re - frain.
Crown Him, crown Him! wor - ship the

King of Sal - va - tion, Shout ho - san - na! Je - sus has come to reign.

# No. 64. When Jesus Came to Bethlehem.

J. B. S.　　　　　　　　　CHILDREN'S SONG.　　　　　　　JOHN B. SHAW.

1. When Je-sus came to Beth-le-hem, And in a man-ger lay,...
2. I go to Him with all my heart And tell Him all I know;
3. And then He makes my heart so glad, He makes me white with-in;...
4. So now I mean to work for Him, And trust Him ev-'ry day,..

The an-gels told the shep-herds where To find Him right a-way....
I say, dear Sav-ior, take my heart, And wash it white as snow...
He takes my naught-y sins a-way. And makes me feel so clean...
Till in His gen-tle arms He takes Me up to heav'n to stay....

CHORUS.

So with the an-gels now I sing His prais-es ev-'ry day,..

And call Him my dear Sav-ior, too, Who took my sins a-way....

Copyright, 1892, by John B. Shaw.

# No. 65.     Treasures in Heaven.

T. C. O'K.

T. C. O'KANE.

1. There's a crown in heav'n for the striv-ing soul, Which the blessed Je-sus Him-
2. There's a joy in heav'n for the mourning soul, Tho' the tears may fall all the
3. There's a home in heav'n for the faith-ful soul, In the ma-ny mansions pre-

self will place On the head of each who shall faith-ful prove, E-ven
earth-ly night; Yet the clouds of sad-ness will break a-way, And re-
pared a-bove, Where the glo-ri-fied shall for-ev-er sing, Of a

**REFRAIN.**

un-to death, in the heav'nly race. Oh, may that crown. . . . . . in heav'n be
                     Oh, may that crown
joic-ing come with the morning light. Oh, may that joy. . . . . . . . . . in heav'n be
                     Oh, may that joy
Sav-ior's free and un-bound-ed love. Oh, may that home. . . . . . . . in heav'n be
                     Oh, may that home

mine,     And I a-mong . . . . . . . the an-gels shine;     Be Thou, O
in heav'n be mine,     And I a-mong     the an-gels shine;

Lord, . . . . . . . my dai-ly guide,        Let me ev-er in Thy love a-bide.
Be Thou, O Lord,     my dai-ly guide,

By permission.

# No. 66.    I am Coming.

E. A. H.

Rev. Elisha A. Hoffman.

1. I am com-ing, Lord, and kneel-ing  At Thy foot-stool low,
2. Sin and guilt in shame con-fess-ing,  At Thy feet I bow;
3. Hear my plea, O bless-ed Sav-ior!  While in tears I bow;
4. Kind-ly, ten-der-ly re-ceive me,  As I hum-bly pray;

And I pray with ten-der feel-ing,  "Oh! save.... me now."
While I lin-ger for the bless-ing,  Oh! save.... me now.
Grant to me Thy grace and fa-vor  Just now,... just now.
Free-ly, gra-cious-ly for-give me  To-day,... to-day.

## CHORUS.

I am com-ing, I am com-ing,  Bless-ed Je-sus, just now;..

Bless and heal me, cleanse and seal me,  I am com-ing just now.

# No. 67.  He Doeth All Things Well.

F. J. BURDETT.

1. Oh, good old way, how sweet thou art! All the way long it is Je - sus;
2. But may our ac - tions al - ways say, All the way long it is Je - sus;
3. This note a - bove the rest shall swell, All the way long it is Je - sus:

May none of us from Thee de - part, All the way long it is Je - sus.
We're marching in the good old way, All the way long it is Je - sus.
That Je - sus do - eth all things well, All the way long it is Je - sus.

**REFRAIN.**

Je - sus, Je - sus, All the way long it is Je - sus;

Je - sus, Je - sus, All the way long it is Je - sus;

# No. 68.    A Story Sweet and True.

E. W. OAKES.    P. BILHORN.

1. We'll sing the won-drous sto-ry, 'Tis ev-er sweet and true,
2. The cru-el world, they took Him, With thorns they crowned His head;
3. His friends whom He loved dear-ly, And whom He died to save,
4. My Lord now reigns in glo-ry. He's com-ing soon for me;

Of Je-sus' love so pre-cious, Now free-ly of-fered you;
And then to Calvary's mount-ain The pre-cious Lamb was led;
They begged His pre-cious bod-y, And laid it in the grave;
And then with all the ran-somed, His glo-rious face I'll see;

He left the joys of heav-en, His Fa-ther's home on high,
The nails of shame were driv-en, The blood flowed from His side;
But God, His Fa-ther, raised Him, Tri-umph-ant, from the dead;
And shout be-hold the bride-groom, Put on your gar-ments fair,

For lost and ru-in'd sin-ners, To suf-fer and to die.....
He cried, O God, for-give them, And bowed His head and died.
Oh, glo-ry hal-le-lu-jah, Now death is cap-tive led.....
And go ye out to meet Him, With rap-ture in the air.....

# No. 69.  The Sunbright Shore.

H. G. JACKSON, D. D.  Arr.

*Moderato.*

1. { There is a land of light and beau-ty— A sun-bright shore,
   { The fade-less tree of life is grow-ing In that fair land,
2. { No night e'er comes to veil the glad-ness, Of that bright clime;
   { There fear no more the heart is keep-ing In chill dis-may,
3. { In - to those realms of bliss su - per - nal, Death can-not come;
   { By faith we see the blest im - mor - tals, Now with Him there,

Where life is love, and joy is du - ty, And sor-row comes no more. )
And ev - er there life's stream is flow-ing, Bright o'er the gold-en sand. )
No win - try blast, no gloom or sad-ness, But one long sum-mer time. )
And there from eyes long used to weep-ing, God wipes all tears a - way. )
And there in mansions bright, e - ter - nal, With Je-sus is our home. )
And soon we'll pass the shin - ing por-tals And in their glo - ry share. )

CHORUS.

We shall meet, no more to sev - er, Loved ones gone be - fore,

And dwell with them in bliss for - ev - er There, on that sunbright shore.

# No. 70. Little Reapers.

*With spirit.*

Rev. J. H. Weber.

1. We are lit - tle reap - ers, Toil - ing thro' the day, Lab'ring in the
2. We are lit - tle reap - ers, In the fields of sin, Striv - ing for the
3. We are lit - tle reap - ers, In the har - vest field, Truth and right the

har - vest O'er the ston - y way; Glean - ing 'mong the this - tles,
Mas - ter Pre - cious souls to win; Point - ing them to Je - sus,
sick - les That we there do wield; And we la - bor ev - er,

**FINE.**

Search-ing thro' the rain, Fit - ting for the gar - ner Bright and gold - en grain.
To the Lamb of God; Fol - low-ing His foot - steps In the paths He trod.
'Neath our Fa - ther's eye, Gath - er - ing the bright sheaves For the home on high.

**CHORUS.**

**D. S. al FINE.**

Toil-ing, toil-ing, toil-ing all the day, Toil - ing, toil-ing in this hap-py way.

# No. 71.     Sunshine in the Soul.

E. E. HEWITT.        JNO. R. SWENEY. By per.

1. There's sun-shine in my soul to - day, More glo - ri - ous and bright
2. There's mu - sic in my soul to - day, A car - ol to my King,
3. There's spring-time in my soul to - day, For when the Lord is near,
4. There's glad-ness in my soul to - day, And hope, and praise, and love,

Than grows in an - y earth - ly sky, For Je - sus is my light.
And Je - sus, list - en - ing can hear The song I can - not sing.
The dove of peace sings in my heart, The flow'rs of grace ap - pear.
For bless-ings which He gives me now, For joys "laid up" a - bove.

**REFRAIN.**

Oh, there's sun - - - shine, Bless - ed sun - - shine,
Oh, there's sun - shine in the soul, Bless - ed sun-shine in the soul,

While the peace - ful, hap - py mo-ments roll; When
hap - py mo-ments roll,

Je - sus shows His smil - ing face There is sun-shine in the soul.

# No. 72.    Let us Hear you Tell It.

J. M. W.

J. M. WHITE.

1. O broth - er, have you told how the Lord for - gave? Let us hear you
2. When toil - ing up the way, was the Sav - ior there? Let us hear you
3. Was ev - er on your tongue such a bless - ed theme? Let us hear you
4. The bat - tles you have fought, and the vic - t'ries won, Let us hear you

tell it o - ver once a - gain; Thy com - ing to the cross, where He
tell it o - ver once a - gain; Did Je - sus bear you up in His
tell it o - ver once a - gain; 'Tis ev - er sweet - er far than the
tell it o - ver once a - gain; 'Twill help them on the way who have

died to save, Let us hear you tell it o - ver once a - gain.
ten - der care? Let us hear you tell it o - ver once a - gain.
sweet - est dream, Let us hear you tell it o - ver once a - gain.
just be - gun, Let us hear you tell it o - ver once a - gain.

Are you walk - ing now in His bless - ed light? Are you cleansed from
Nev - er have you found such a friend as He, Who can help you
There are ach - ing hearts in the world's great throng, Who have sought for
We are striv - ing now with the hosts of sin, Soon with Christ our

ev - 'ry guilt - y stain? Is He your joy by day, and your
'midst the toil and pain; Oh, all the world should hear what He's
rest, and all in vain: Hold Je - sus up to them by your
Sav - ior we shall reign; Ye ran - somed of the Lord, try a

# Let us Hear you Tell It. Concluded.

song by night? Let us hear you tell it o - ver once a - gain.
done for thee; Let us hear you tell it o - ver once a - gain.
word and song; Let us hear you tell it o - ver once a - gain.
soul to win; Let us hear you tell it o - ver once a - gain.

**CHORUS.**

Let us hear you tell it o - ver,
Let us hear you tell it o - ver once a - gain,

tell it o - ver once a - gain.
tell it o - ver, tell it o - ver once a - gain,

Tell the sweet and bless - ed sto - ry, It will help you on to

glo - ry, Let us hear you tell it o - ver once a - gain.

# No. 74.    The Best Friend is Jesus.

P. P. B.

P. P. Bilhorn.

Duet. Sop. (or Ten.) & Alto.

1. Oh, the best friend to have is Je - sus, When the cares of life up-
2. What a friend I have found in Je - sus! Peace and com - fort to my
3. Tho' I pass thro' the night of sor - row, And the chill - y waves of
4. When at last to our home we gath - er, With the loved ones who have

on you roll; He will heal the wound - ed heart, He will
soul He brings; Lean-ing on His might - y arm, I will
Jor - dan roll, Nev - er need I shrink nor fear, For my
gone be - fore, We will sing up - on the shore, Prais - ing

strength and grace im - part; Oh, the best friend to have is Je - sus.
fear no ill nor harm; Oh, the best friend to have is Je - sus.
Sav - ior is so near; Oh, the best friend to have is Je - sus.
Him for ev - er - more; Oh, the best friend to have is Je - sus.

# The Best Friend is Jesus. Concluded.

CHORUS. *Spirited.*

The best friend to have is Je - - - - sus, The best friend to have is
Je - sus ev - 'ry day,

Je - - - - - sus, He will help you when you fall, He will
Je - sus all the way;

hear you when you call; Oh, the best friend to have is Je - sus.

# No. 75.    Jesus, Savior, Pilot Me.

J. E. GOULD.

FINE.

1. Je - sus, Sav - ior, pi - lot me, O - ver life's tem-pest-uous sea;
D.C.—*Chart and com - pass came from Thee: Je - sus, Sav - ior, pi - lot me.*

D.C.

Unknown waves be - fore me roll, Hid - ing rocks and treacherous shoal;

2 As a mother stills her child,
Thou canst hush the ocean wild;
Boisterous waves obey Thy will
When Thou say'st to them, "Be still!"
Wondrous Sovereign of the sea,
Jesus, Savior, pilot me.

3 When at last I near the shore,
And the fearful breakers roar,
'Twixt me and the peaceful rest,
Then while leaning on Thy breast,
May I hear Thee say to me,
"Fear not, I will pilot thee!"

# No. 76. The Way of the Cross.

E. W. BLANDY.                                             Arr. by J. S. NORRIS.

*Andantino con espressione.*

1. I can hear my Sav - ior call-ing, I can hear my Sav - ior call-ing,
2. I'll go with Him thro' the gar-den, I'll go with Him thro' the gar-den,
3. I'll go with Him thro' the judgment, I'll go with Him thro' the judgment,
4. He will give me grace and glo - ry, He will give me grace and glo - ry,

I can hear my Sav - ior call-ing, "Take thy cross and fol-low, fol - low me."
I'll go with Him thro' the gar-den, I'll go with Him, with Him all the way.
I'll go with Him thro' the judgment, I'll go with Him, with Him all the way.
He will give me grace and glo-ry, And go with me, with me all the way.

CHORUS.

1-3. Where He leads me I will fol - low, Where He leads me I will fol - low,
4. Yes, He gives me grace and glo - ry, Yes, He gives me grace and glo - ry,

FINAL CHORUS.

As He leads me I do fol - low, As He leads me I do fol - low,

Where He leads me I will fol - low, I'll go with Him, with Him all the way.
Yes, He gives me grace and glo - ry, And goes with me, with me all the way.
As He leads me I do fol - low, He goes with me, with me all the way.

Copyright, 1889, by J. S. Norris. By per.

# No. 77. There's Music in My Soul!

Rev. HENRY BURTON.

JOSHUA GILL.

1. The world is full of sing-ing. I hear it ev-'ry-where; The flow'rs their bells are
2. My heart was fond of sigh-ing. With just some breaks of song: As self was ev-er
3. My life was full of sad-ness, Of o-ver-weighting care: But now the soil of
4. And so my heart keeps clinging To the dear Master's Word; And it is al-ways

ring-ing Out on the scent-ed air: And up a-bove, a-round me, The
try-ing To make its weak-ness strong; But now in Him con-fid ing, His
glad-ness Has turn'd to praise the prayer. And so I keep pur-su-ing, And
sing-ing Just like a spring-time bird: I know not what the harps be, Where

si-lent anthems roll: The glorious Lord has found me. There's mu-sic in my soul!
Word has made me whole. And e'er in Christ a-bid-ing, There's mu-sic in my soul!
pressing t'ward the goal: But praying, waiting, do-ing. There's mu-sic in my soul!
heavenly anthems roll; I know that heav'n is near me. There's mu-sic in my soul!

## CHORUS.

The blood of Christ is flow-ing, Its waves a-round me roll;

My heart with love is glow-ing, There's mu-sic in my soul!

# No. 78.   Is My Name Written There?

M. A. K.                                         FRANK M. DAVIS.

1. Lord, I care not for rich - es, Neith - er sil - ver nor gold;
2. Lord, my sins they are ma - ny, Like the sands of the sea,
3. Oh! that beau - ti - ful cit - y, With its man - sions of light,

I would make sure of heav - en, I would en - ter the fold;
But Thy blood, O my Sav - ior, Is suf - fi - cient for me;
With its glo - ri - fied be - ings, In pure gar - ments of white;

In the book of Thy king - dom, With its pa - ges so fair,
For Thy prom - ise is writ - ten, In bright let - ters that glow,
Where no e - vil thing com - eth, To de - spoil what is fair;

Tell me, Je - sus, my Sav - ior, Is my name writ - ten there?
"Tho' your sins be as scar - let, They shall be white as snow."
Where the an - gels are watch - ing, Is my name writ - ten there?

REFRAIN.

Is my name writ - ten there, On the page white and fair?

By permission.

# Is My Name Written There? Concluded.

In the book of Thy king - dom, Is my name writ - ten there?

## No. 79.    Step Out on the Promise.

MAGGIE POTTER.   Arr. by E. F. M.                                    E. F. MILLER.

1. O mourn-er in Zi - on, how bless - ed art thou.` For Je - sus is
2. O ye that are hun-gry and thirst - y, re - joice! For ye shall be
3. Who sighs for a heart from in - iq - ui - ty free? O, poor trou-bled
4. Step out on this prom-ise, and Christ thou shalt win, "The blood of His

wait - ing to com - fort thee now, Fear not to re - ly on the
filled; do you hear that sweet voice In - vit - ing you now to the
soul! there's a prom - ise for thee, There's rest, wea - ry one, in the
Son cleans-eth us from all sin," It cleans - eth me now, hal - le -

word - of thy God; Step out on the prom-ise,—get un - der the blood.
ban-quet of God; Step out on the prom-ise,—get un - der the blood.
bo - som of God; Step out on the prom-ise,—get un - der the blood.
lu - jah to God; I rest on His prom-ise,—I'm un - der the blood.

# No. 80. Over in the Glory-Land.

C. H. G.

CHAS. H. GABRIEL.

1. We are on our way to a home on high, O-ver in the glo-ry-land;
2. We will join the song that the ransomed sing, O-ver in the glo-ry-land;
3. When the cares and tri-als of earth are past,—O-ver in the glo-ry-land;
4. With the lov'd ones gone to that shin-ing shore, O-ver in the glo-ry-land;

There we'll meet and rest, in the by and by, O-ver in the glo-ry-land.
And for-ev-er praise our e-ter-nal King, O-ver in the glo-ry-land.
Je-sus waits to crown us His own at last, O-ver in the glo-ry-land.
We shall meet, oh, joy, meet to part no more, O-ver in the glo-ry-land.

**CHORUS.**

O-ver in the glo-ry-land! O-ver in the glo-ry-land! There with

all the blest we shall meet and rest, O-ver in the glo-ry-land.

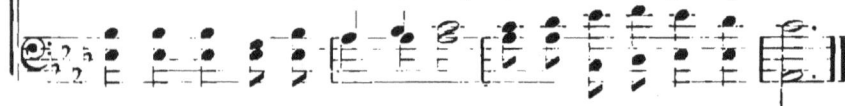

# No. 81. Walking in Love.

ABBIE MILLS.     W. S. NICKLE.

1. Walk-ing in love, on my jour-ney I go, Care-ful for noth-ing but
2. Walk-ing in love, I am find-ing sup-plies Sweet, and so fresh from the
3. Love nev-er fail-eth, its springs are on high; Hearts 'neath the fountain can
4. Walk-ing in love is but walk-ing with God; Saints of all a-ges, this

how I may show How much I love Him who gives me His peace,
prayer-o-pened skies, Strengthened with might by His glo-ri-ous grace,
nev-er be dry, Brim-o-ver full-ness so cost-ly, so free,
path-way have trod, Quick-'ning their pace at the bright hour of ev'n,

Sign-ing in crim-son the sin-ner's re-lease.
Pa-tient and joy-ful His will I em-brace.
Seeks for a chan-nel thro' you and thro' me.
Sweeping a-long thro' the gates in-to heav'n.

**CHORUS.**

Walking in love; Are you walk-ing in love, Step-keeping step to the mu-sic a-bove? Glo-ry, and bless-ing, sal-va-tion and might, This is their song, in the land of de-light.

# No. 82.　　Secret Prayer.

ABBIE MILLS.　　　　　　　　　　　　　　　　　　　　W. S. NICKLE.

1. Joy di-vine I now am find-ing, As I kneel be-fore the throne,
2. In the dawn-ing light of morn-ing, Haste I to the mer-cy-seat:
3. When the noontide cares op-press me, And the world for-bids me rest,
4. Wea-ry, 'mid the shades of ev-'ning, Sigh-ing o-ver tri-als strong,
5. In the light and in the shad-ow, All the time and ev-'ry-where,

In the hour of sweet com-mun-ion When shut in with God a-lone.
Bright-er than the ris-ing sun-beam Is the glo-ry 'round His feet!
Then I breathe the pray'r un-spok-en, While I lean up-on His breast.
Then I feel His arm be-neath me, And my heart is filled with song.
I am need-ing this com-mun-ion Found a-lone in se-cret pray'r.

**CHORUS.**

Oh! how bless-ed is com-mun-ion With my Je-sus, Sav-ior, King!

When I hear His voice so ten-der, And I tell Him ev-'ry-thing.

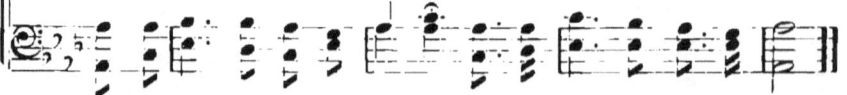

Copyright, 1894, by W. S. Nickle.

# No. 83. Bring Me Still Closer to Thee.

J. S. N.  J. S. Norris.

*Andantino.*

1. Graut me Thy spir-it, dear Sav-ior, Fount-ain of meek-ness and love;..
2. Give me Thy mind, bless-ed Sav-ior, Help me to "walk in the light;"
3. Give me Thy beau-ty, dear Sav-ior, Show me Thy glo-ry di-vine;

Gra-cious-ly guide and up-hold me, Bring me to man-sions a-bove.
True to all truth ev-er make me, So shall my path-way be bright.
Dwell-ing with-in, make me ra-diant, So that for Thee I may shine.

**CHORUS.**

Hear Thou my prayer, lov-ing Sav-ior, Clos-er to Thee would I be;...

What-ev-er else Thou de-ny-est, Bring me still clos-er to Thee.

# No. 84.  Jesus Calls Me.

M. L. McPhail.

Sop. and Alto Duet.

1. An - y - where that Je - sus calls me, An - y work He gives to do.
2. Oh, the bless - ed - ness of trust - ing, And the full heart sat - is - fied!
3. Peace, a - bid - ing, like a riv - er Rest, the world can nev - er know;
4. All my soul is filled with bless - ing While I sit at Thy dear feet;
5. If the way be rough and thorn - y, Thou didst tread the same for me;

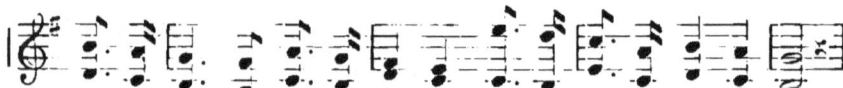

An - y tri - al or af - flic - tion He may call me to pass through,
Oh, the ho - ly joy of lov - ing On - ly Him the cru - ci - fied!
Faith, that sees a pity - ing Fa - ther Where - so - e'er the feet may go:—
And a con - scious-ness of serv - ing Makes the hal-lowed cross more sweet,
Shall the serv - ant than the Mas - ter More ex - empt from tri - al be?

My glad heart has the as - sur - ance He will help me bear and do,
Look-ing up with faith un - wav - 'ring To the wounds in His dear side,
Love up - ris - ing, fill - ing, sweet-'ning Ev - 'ry cup of pain and woe,
While I own Thy full sal - va - tion And the cleans-ing all com-plete,
If I may at last be - hold Thee, It will be e - nough for me,

My glad heart has the as - sur - ance He will help me bear and do.
Look-ing up with faith un - wav - 'ring To the wounds in His dear side.
Love up - ris - ing, fill - ing, sweet-'ning Ev - 'ry cup of pain and woe.
While I own Thy full sal - va - tion And the cleans-ing all com-plete.
If I may at last be - hold Thee, It will be e - nough for me.

CHORUS.

An - y - where that Je - sus calls me, An - y work He gives to do,

An - y tri - al or af - flic - tion He may call me to pass through.

# No. 85. God Loves His Own.

C. H. G.

CHAS. H. GABRIEL.

1. God loves His own as the shep-herd His sheep! Faith-ful is He from all
2. God loves His own—what a glo - ri - ous thought! For by the blood of His
3. God loves His own! oh, ye na - tions a - wake! For, as He lives, He will

dan - ger to keep: With His al - might - y arm He will up - hold,
Son we were bought; In His pa - vil - ion we safe - ly may hide,
nev - er for - sake. He'll be a friend when all oth - ers have flown,—

**CHORUS.**

Shield them and car - ry them safe to the fold.
Un - der His wing may se - cure - ly a - bide.   } Sing hal-le - lu - jah, the
Praise Him for - ev - er. He lov - eth His own.

*Ritard. . . . . A tempo.*

ti - dings pro-claim! Let ev-'ry thing that hath breath, praise His name! Tell the glad

sto - ry a - gain and a - gain, God loves His own, hal-le - lu - jah! A - men!

## No. 86.　　That Beautiful City of Gold.

DUET.

Rev. J. S. NORRIS.

1. There's a cit - y that looks o'er the val - ley of death, And its
2. There the King, our Re - deem - er, the Lord whom we love, Will the
3. Ev - 'ry soul we have led to the foot of the cross, Ev - 'ry
4. There sick - ness and sor - row, and death are un-known; There

glo - ries may nev - er be told; ...... There the sun nev-er sets, and the
faith - ful with rap-ture be - hold; ...... There the right - eous for - ev - er shall
lamb we have brought to the fold, ...... Will be kept as bright jew-els our
glo - ries ou glo - ries un - fold; ...... There the Lamb is the light in the

leaves nev - er fade, In that beau - ti - ful Cit - y of gold..........
shine as the stars, In that beau - ti - ful Cit - y of gold..........
crowns to a - dorn, In that beau - ti - ful Cit - y of gold..........
midst of the throne, In that beau - ti - ful Cit - y of gold..........

CHORUS.

Beau - ti - ful, ......
Cit - y of gold,
Beau - ti - ful, Beau - ti - ful, Beau - ti - ful, Beau - ti - ful

Copyright, 1892, by W. S. Nickle.

# That Beautiful City of Gold. Concluded.

Beau - ti - ful,........

Cit - y of gold;........... Beau - ti - ful, Beau - ti - ful,

*Repeat last time pp.*

Cit - y of gold.

Beau - ti - ful, Half of it nev - er.... was told......

## No. 87.　Jesus Christ is Passing by.

" He heard that it was Jesus of Nazareth. "　Mark. 10: 47.

J. DENHAM SMITH.　　　　　　　　　　　　MRS. JOS. F. KNAPP.

1. Je - sus Christ is pass - ing by,..　Sin - ner lift to Him thine eye;..
2. Lo! He stands and calls to thee,　"What wilt thou then have of me?"
3. "Lord, I would Thy mer - cy see;...　Lord, re - veal Thy love to me;...
4. Oh, how sweet the touch of pow - er Comes,—and is sal - va - tion's hour.

*Rit.*

As the pre - cious mo - ments flee,　Cry, be mer - ci - ful to me!
Rise, and tell Him all Thy need;　Rise, He call - eth thee in - deed.
Let it pen - e - trate my soul,　All my heart and life con - trol.
Je - sus gives from guilt re - lease,　"Faith hath saved thee, go in peace!"

By permission.

## No. 88.  Come to the Mercy Seat.

H. G. Jackson, D. D.

W. S. Nickle.

1. Come, sin-ner, to the mer-cy seat, Come, sin-ner, to the mer-cy seat;
2. Just as you are, come now to Him, Just as you are, come now to Him;
3. Re-pent, be-lieve in Je-sus' name, Re-pent, be-lieve in Je-sus' name;
4. His pre-cious blood for you He shed, His pre-cious blood for you He shed;

Come, sin-ner, to the mer-cy seat; 'Tis Je-sus bids you come...
Just as you are, come now to Him, His blood will make you clean ..
Re-pent, be-lieve in Je-sus' name, And you shall be for-giv'n...
His pre-cious blood for you He shed, Your sins to wash a-way....

CHORUS.

O won-der-ful Sav-ior! O bless-ed Re-deem-er!

O won-der-ful Sav--ior, He longs to save you now!..

5 A full atonement Jesus made,
A full atonement Jesus made,
A full atonement Jesus made,
For you on Calvary.
Cho —O wonderful Savior! etc.

6 No longer doubt, but trust His word,
No longer doubt, but trust His word,
No longer doubt, but trust His word,
And He will save you now.
Cho.—O wonderful Savior! etc.

# No. 89. The Port of Peace.

Rev. H. G. Jackson, D. D.  Miss Emma E. Meyer.

1. We are on the o - cean sail - ing, Toss'd on life's tu - mult-uous waves,
2. In the lu - rid sky a - bove us, Faith can see no bea - con star,
3. Thus the Twelve, midst an - gry bil - lows, Struggled long on Gal - i - lee,
4. Let the storm rage ne'er so wild - ly, Be the har - bor far or near,

Night and dark - ness all a - round us, While the tem - pest fierce - ly raves.
But our Pi - lot will con - vey us Safe - ly o'er the har - bor bar.
Till the Sav - ior, roused from slumber, Spake and calmed the troub-led sea.
If we on - ly sail with Je - sus, We have nev - er cause to fear.

**CHORUS.**

Soon the storms will all be o - ver, All our dark fore-bod - ings cease;—

Home at last, we'll soon cast an - chor Safe with - in the Port of Peace.

# No. 90. I will Shout His Praise in Glory.

P. H. DINGMAN.

JNO. R. SWENEY.

1. You ask what makes me happy, my heart so free from care, It is because my
2. I was a friendless wand'rer till Je-sus took me in; My life was full of
3. I wish that ev-'ry sin-ner before His throne would bow; He waits to bid them
4. I mean to live for Je-sus while here on earth I stay, And when His voice shall

Sav - ior in mer-cy heard my pray'r; He brought me out of dark - ness and
sor - row, my heart was full of sin; But when the blood so pre-cious spoke
wel-come, He longs to bless them now; If they but knew the rapt - ure that
call me to realms of end - less day, As one by one we gath - er, re -

now the light I see; O bless-ed, lov-ing Sav-ior! to Him the praise shall be.
par - don to my soul; Oh, bliss-ful, blissful moment! 'twas joy be-yond con-trol.
in His love I see, They'd come and shout sal-va-tion, and sing His praise with me.
joic-ing on the shore, We'll shout His praise in glory, and sing for-ev - er-more.

**CHORUS.**

I will shout His praise in glo - ry,..............
So will I, so will I,
And we'll

all sing hal-le - lu - jah in heav-en by and by; I will shout His praise in

## I will Shout His Praise.—Concluded.

glo - ry,........  And we'll all sing halle-lu-jah  in heaven by and by.
So will I, so will I,

---

No. 91.  **Oh, Happy Day.**

E. F. RIMBAULT.

1. { Oh, hap - py day, that fixed my choice On Thee, my Sav - ior, and my God! }
{ Well may this glow-ing heart re - joice, And tell its rapt - ures all a - broad. }

**CHORUS.**  FINE.

Hap - py day, hap - py day, When Je - sus washed my sins a - way;

D. S.

He taught me how to watch and pray, And live re - joic - ing ev - 'ry day.

2 'Tis done, the great transaction's done;
I am the Lord's and He is mine;
He drew me and I follow'd on,
  Charmed to confess the voice divine.

3 Now rest, my long divided heart!
Fixed on this blissful centre, rest;
Nor ever from thy Lord depart,
  With Him, of every good possessed.

# No. 92. Scattering Precious Seed.

W. A. OGDEN.     GEO. C. HUGG.

1. Scat - ter - ing pre - cious seed by the way - side, Scat - ter - ing
2. Scat - ter - ing pre - cious seed for the grow - ing, Scat - ter - ing
3. Scat - ter - ing pre - cious seed, doubt-ing nev - er, Scat - ter - ing

pre - cious seed by the hill - side; Scat - ter - ing pre - cious seed
pre - cious seed, free - ly sow - ing; Scat - ter - ing pre - cious seed,
pre - cious seed, trust-ing ev - er; Sow - ing the word with pray'r

o'er the field wide, Scat - ter - ing pre - cious seed by the way.
trust-ing, know - ing, Sure - ly the Lord will send it the rain.
and en - deav - or, Trust-ing the Lord for growth and for yield.

CHORUS.

Sow - - ing in the morn - - ing, Sow - - ing
Sow-ing the precious seed, Sowing the precious seed, Sow-ing the seed at noon-

at the noon - - - tide, Sow - - ing in the
tide, Sow-ing the pre-cious seed, Sow-ing the pre-cious seed,

## Scattering Precious Seed. Concluded.

*pp*

ev - - 'ning, Sow-ing the pre-cious seed by the way..........
Sowing the precious seed, by the way.

## No. 93. Preciousness of Jesus.

JOHN NEWTON.     LEWIS EDSON.

1. How te - dious and taste-less the hours When Je - sus no long - er I see!
2. His name yields the rich - est per-fume, And sweet - er than mu - sic His voice;
3. Con-tent with be - hold - ing His face, My all to His pleas-ure re-signed,

FINE.

Sweet prospects, sweet birds, and sweet flow'rs, Have all lost their sweet-ness to me;
His pres-ence dis - pers - es my gloom, And makes all with - in me re-joice;
No changes of sea - son or place Would make a - ny change in my mind:

D. S. But when I am hap - py in Him, De - cem - ber 's as pleas-ant as May.
No mor - tal so hap - py as I, My sum-mer would last all the year.
And pris-ons would pal - ac - es prove, If Je - sus would dwell with me there.

D. S.

The mid-sum - mer sun shines but dim, The fields strive in vain to look gay;
I should, were He al - ways thus nigh, Have noth-ing to wish or to fear.
While blest with a sense of His love, A pal - ace a toy would ap - pear.

# No. 94. Nobody Knows but Jesus.

R. M. OFFORD.                                                                    J. J. LOWE.

1. No - bod - y knows the bur-dens I bear, No - bod - y knows but Je - sus,
2. No - bod - y knows the troub-le I see, No - bod - y knows but Je - sus,
3. No - bod - y knows how tempted I am, No - bod - y knows but Je - sus,
4. No - bod - y knows the sor-row I feel, No - bod - y knows but Je - sus,
5. Help me to sing His mer-cy and grace, Help me to sing of Je - sus,

No - bod - y helps me to car-ry my cares, No-bod - y helps like Je - sus,
Won-der-ful com-fort is Christ to me, No-bod - y helps like Je - sus,
He can de - liv - er, blest be His name, Might-y to save is Je - sus,
Grief can-not be that He can - not heal, No-bod - y soothes like Je - sus,
Soon shall we meet be - fore His dear face, Soon shall we meet with Je - sus,

CHORUS.

Oh! I tell Him all my grief, Tell it all to Je - sus,

He doth give me sweet re - lief, Je - sus, bless - ed Je - sus.

Copyright transferred 1893 to P. P. Bilhorn. By per. from "Crowning Glory Revised."

# No. 95. The Love and Power of Jesus.

ABBIE MILLS.                                                    WALTER A. KELLER.

1. Sing the love and pow'r of Je - sus, Have you not new treas-ure found?
2. Sing the love and pow'r of Je - sus, Have you grace e - nough to - day?
3. Sing the love and pow'r of Je - sus, On the mount or in the vale;
4. Sing the love and pow'r of Je - sus, Are your gar-ments clean and white?

Ten-der mer - cies of the morn-ing, Scatt'ring glo - ry all a - round?
To the store-house nev - er emp - ty, Have you found the promised way?
Are you day by day vic - to - rious? In His might do you pre - vail?
Are you read - y for the cit - y, Hav-ing Je - sus for its light?

CHORUS.

Sing the love and pow'r of Je - sus, Let the hal - le - lu - jahs roll;

Je - sus, Je - sus, wondrous Sav - ior, Oh, what mu - sic to the soul!

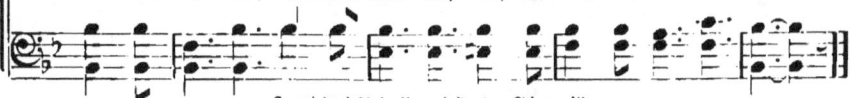

# No. 96. Throw Out the Life-Line.

*(May be sung as a Solo and Chorus.)*

Rev. E. S. Ufford.  E. S. U. Arr. by Geo. C. Stebbins.

1. Throw out the Life-Line a-cross the dark wave, There is a broth-er whom
2. Throw out the Life-Line with hand quick and strong: Why do you tar - ry, why
3. Throw out the Life-Line to dan-ger-fraught men, Sink - ing in an-guish where
4. Soon will the sea - son of res - cue be o'er, Soon will they drift to e -

some one should save: Some-bod - y's broth-er! oh, who then, will dare To
lin - ger so long? See! he is sink-ing; oh, hast - en to - day—And
you've nev - er been: Winds of temp - ta - tion and bil - lows of woe Will
ter - ni - ty's shore, Haste, then, my broth-er, no time for de - lay, But

### CHORUS.

throw out the Life-Line, his per - il to share?
out with the Life-Boat! a - way, then, a - way!  } Throw out the Life-Line!
soon hurl them out where the dark wa - ters flow.
throw out the Life-Line and save them to - day.

Throw out the Life-Line! Some one is drift - ing a - way; Throw out the

Life-Line! Throw out the Life-Line! Some one is sinking to - day.

# No. 97. For You and For Me.

W. L. T.

WILL L. THOMPSON.

*Very Slow.* pp

1. Soft - ly and ten-der - ly  Je-sus  is  call-ing,  Call-ing for you and for me;
2. Why should we tarry when Je-sus  is  pleading,  Pleading for you and for me;
3. Time is now fleeting, the moments are passing,  Pass-ing for you and for me;
4. Oh, for the won-der-ful love He has promis'd,  Promis'd for you and for me;

See on the por-tals He's waiting and watching,  Watching for you and for me.
Why should we linger and heed not His mercies,  Mer-cies for you and for me?
Shadows are gather-ing. death-beds are coming.  Com-ing for you and for me.
Tho' we have sinned He has mercy and par-don,  Par-don for you and for me.

## CHORUS.

*Cres.*

Come home,..... Come home;..... Ye who are wea-ry, come home;.....
Come home,  Come home,

pp  ppp  *Rit.*  pp

Earnest-ly, ten-der - ly, Je-sus is call-ing, Call-ing, O sin-ner, come home!

By per. of Will L. Thompson & Co., E. Liverpool, & Chicago, Ill.

# No. 98. Are You Ready?

Naomi Quincy.

J. S. Norris.

Solo. Soprano or Tenor.

1. Are you read - y? Are you read-y?.... If the Son of man should come?
2. Have you list - ened to His coun-sel.... And o-beyed His gra-cious word?
3. Would He gird Him - self and bid you... With His faith-ful ones sit down?

Would you hear His com - men - da - tion,.. In those bless-ed words, "Well done?"
Are your loins all gird - ed read-y.... To go out to meet the Lord?
Would He deign, Him-self, to deck you.. With a glitt'r-ing, fade - less crown?

For He says that He is com-ing,.. On His aw - ful throne of state;
If He came, would He now find you.. With a lamp that's burn-ing bright?
Since you know not when He's com-ing,— With your lamp well filled and bright,

O how blest will be that ser - vant.. Who doth for His com - ing wait!
Would you glad - ly hear the sum-mons If He called for you to-night?
Be ye read - y for His pres - ence, For the Lord may come to-night.

CHORUS.

Are you read - y?.............. Are you read - y? ... ............
Are you read-y? Are you read-y?

## Are You Ready? Concluded.

*Rit.  Cres.*

With a lamp that's burn-ing bright?..... Be ye read-y!..............
burning bright?            Be ye read - y!

Be ye read - y!............. For—per - haps He'll come to - night.
Be ye read-y!

No. 99.        I Do Believe.

C. WESLEY

1. Fa - ther, I stretch my hands to Thee; No oth - er help I know;
2. What did Thine on - ly Son en - dure Be - fore I drew my breath!
3. Au - thor of faith, to Thee I lift My wea - ry, long - ing eyes;

CHO.—*I do be - lieve, I now be - lieve That Je - sus died for me;*

If Thou with-draw Thy - self from me, Ah, whith-er shall I go?
With pain, with la - bor, to se - cure My soul from end - less death?
O, may I now re - ceive that gift; My soul, with - out it, d ies.

*And thro' His blood, His pre-cious blood, I shall from sin be free.*

## No. 100.    He Takes My Sin Away.

C. ELLIOTT.

F. E. H.

1. Just as I am, with-out one plea, But that Thy blood was shed for me,
2. Just as I am, and wait-ing not To rid my soul of one dark blot;
3. Just as I am, tho' toss'd a - bout With many a con - flict, many a doubt;
4. Just as I am, poor, wretched, blind, Sight, riches, heal - ing of the mind,
5. Just as I am, Thou wilt re-ceive, Wilt wel-come, par - don, cleanse, re-lieve,
6. Just as I am, Thy love un-known Hath bro - ken ev - 'ry bar - rier down;

And that Thou bid'st me come to Thee, O Lamb of God, I come!
To Thee, whose blood can cleanse each spot, O Lamb of God, I come!
Fightings with - in, and foes with-out, O Lamb of God, I come!
Yea, all I need in Thee to find, O Lamb of God, I come!
Be - cause Thy prom - ise I be - lieve, O Lamb of God, I come!
Now to be Thine, and Thine a - lone, O Lamb of God, I come!

CHORUS.

He takes my sin a - way, He takes my sin a - way,

Thou spot-less Lamb, Thy precious blood Takes all my sin a - way.

Copyright, 1891, by Joshua Gill. By per.

# No. 101. Satisfied with Jesus.

E. S. L.

Rev. E. S. Lorenz.

1. I am walk-ing with the Sav-ior in the bless-ed nar-row way, I am
2. In my grief He's con-sol-a-tion, in my tri-als He's my stay, I am
3. When I fal-ter in my weakness, on His arm He bids me lean, I am

sat-is-fied with Christ, my Lord; Once my soul was in the darkness; now has
sat-is-fied with Christ, my Lord; With His ten-der arms a-round me, I can
sat-is-fied with Christ, my Lord; When temp-ta-tions o-ver-whelm me, with His

*D. S.—nev-er will for-sake me, but will*

FINE.

dawned the gold-en day, I am sat-is-fied with Christ, my Lord.
nev-er know dis-may, I am sat-is-fied with Christ, my Lord.
blood He makes me clean, I am sat-is-fied with Christ, my Lord.

*ev-er be my guide, I am sat-is-fied with Christ, my Lord.*

CHORUS.

I am sat-is-fied, yes, I am sat-is-fied,
I am sat-is-fied with Je-sus, I am sat-is-fied with Je-sus,

D. S.

I am sat-is-fied to walk with Him the long, long way. For He

# No. 102.  He is Able to Deliver Thee.

W. A. O.                                                                W. A. OGDEN.

1. 'Tis the grand - est theme thro' the a - ges rung; 'Tis the
2. 'Tis the grand - est theme in the earth or main; 'Tis the
3. 'Tis the grand - est theme, let the ti - dings roll, To the

grand - est theme for a mor - tal tongue, 'Tis the
grand - est theme for a mor - tal strain, 'Tis the
guilt - y heart, to the sin - ful soul, Look to

grand - est theme that the world e'er sung, "Our
grand - est theme tell the world a - gain, "Our
God in faith, He will make thee whole, "Our

God is a - ble to de - liv - er thee."

**CHORUS.**

He is a - - - ble to de - liv - er thee, He is
a - ble, He is a - ble,

# He is Able to Deliver Thee. Concluded.

a - - - - - ble to de - liv - er thee; Tho' by sin op - prest, Go to
a - ble, He is a - ble

Him for rest; Our God is a - ble to de - liv - er thee.

## No. 103.    Turn to The Lord.

JOSEPH HEART. 1759.                                          ANON. 1830.

FINE.

1. { Come, ye sin - ners, poor and need - y, Weak and wound-ed, sick and sore; }
   { Je - sus read - y stands to save you, Full of pit - y, love and pow'r. }

D. C. Glo - ry, hon - or, and sal - va - tion, Christ, the Lord, has come to reign.

CHORUS.                                                        D. C.

Turn to the Lord and seek sal - va - tion, Sound the praise of His dear name;

2 Now, ye needy, come and welcome,
    God's free bounty glorify;
  True belief and true repentance,
    Every grace that brings you nigh.

3 Let not conscience make you linger,
    Nor of fitness fondly dream;

All the fitness He requireth,
  Is to feel your need of Him.

4 Come, ye weary, heavy-laden,
    Bruised and mangled by the fall,
  If you tarry till you're better,
    You will never come at all.

# No. 104. Send the Light.

C. H. G.

C. H. G

1. There's a call comes ring-ing o'er the rest-less wave, "Send the light!........
2. We have heard the Ma-ce-do-nian call to-day, "Send the light!........
3. Let us pray that grace may ev-'ry-where abound, Send the light!........
4. Let us not grow wea-ry in the work of love, Send the light!........

Send the light!

Send the light!" There are souls to res-cue, there are
Send the light!" And a gold-en off-'ring at the
Send the light! And a Christ-like spir-it ev-'ry-
Send the light! Send the light! Let us gath-er jew-els for a

souls to save, Send the light!.......... Send the light!..........
cross we lay,
where be found,
crown a-bove, Send the light! Send the light!

CHORUS. *The first eight measures, (or Bass Solo,) may be omitted.*

We will spread the ev-er-last-ing light,

We will spread.......... the ev-er-last-ing light With a

BASS SOLO.

# Send the Light. Concluded.

With a will - ing, will-ing heart and hand, Giving God the
will - - ing heart and hand,............ Giv-ing God....... the glo-ry

glo - ry ev - er-more, We will fol - low, fol - low His command.
ev - - er - more, We will fol - low His com - mand...............

Send the light,........... the bless-ed gos - pel light, Let it
Send the light, the bless - ed gos - pel light,

shine....... from shore to shore!.......... Send the light!..... and let its
Let it shine from shore to shore! Send the light! and

ra - diant beams Light the world...... for - ev - er - more............
let its radiant beams Light the world for - ev - er-more.

# No. 105.      Tell It Out!

F. R. HAVERGAL.

J. H. HALL.

1. Tell it out a-mong the peo-ple that the Lord is King!      Tell it out!

2. Tell it out a-mong the peo ple that the Savior reigns! Tell it out!...... Tell it

3. Tell it out a-mong the peo-ple, Je - sus reigns a-bove!      Tell it out!

Tell it out! Tell it out a-mong the na-tions, bid them shout and sing!

out!      Tell it out a-mong the heath-en, bid them break their chains! Tell it

Tell it out! Tell it out a-mong the heath-en that His reign is love!

Tell it out! Tell it out! Tell it out with ad-or - a-tion that He shall increase!

out!      Tell it out! Tell it out among the weeping ones that Jesus lives! Tell it

Tell it out! Tell it out! Tell it out among the highways and the lanes at home!

# Tell It Out. Concluded.

Tell it out! Tell it out! That the mighty King of glo-ry is the

out! Tell it out! Tell it out a-mong the wea-ry ones, the

Tell it out! Tell it out! Let it ring across the mountains and the

King of peace! Tell it out! Tell it out! Tell it

rest He gives! Tell it out! Tell it out! Tell it

o - cean's foam! Tell it out! Tell it out! That the

out with ju - bi - la - tion, let the song in-crease! Tell it out! Tell it out!

out a-mong the sin-ners that He came to save! Tell it out!...... Tell it out!

wea - ry, heav-y la-den need no long-er roam! Tell it out! Tell it out!

# No. 106.     For Jesus' Sake.

Dedicated to Lucy Rider Meyer.

Rev. WILLIAM FAWCETT, D. D.           NELLIE E. W. FAWCETT.

1. "For Je-sus' sake;" thus *an - gels* sing A-round the great white
2. "For Je-sus' sake," the *blood - washed* shout! All safe-ly sealed in
3. "For Je-sus' sake" shall be *our* theme; His love, our rich-est
4. "For Je-sus' sake;" O bless-ed One! Ful-fill our heart's de-

throne; To Him their rich - est off'r-ings bring, And wor-ship Him a-
heav'n; They sing of His re - deem-ing blood, Thro' which they were for-
prize; For His dear name a - lone we'll live, And by His pow'r a-
sire; We would un - to Thy glo - ry live, And in Thy work ex-

lone; And wor-ship Him a - lone, And wor - ship Him a - lone.
a-lone,           a-lone,
giv'n; Thro' which they were for-giv'n, Thro' which they were for-giv'n.
for-giv'n,         for-giv'n,
rise; And by His pow'r a-rise, And by His pow'r a - rise.
a - rise.         a - rise,
pire; And in Thy work ex - pire, And in Thy work ex - pire.
ex-pire,        ex-pire,

**CHORUS.**

"*For Je - sus' sake*" shall be our song! His right in us we

His

Copyright, 1892, by Nellie E. Whipple Fawcett. By per.

# For Jesus' Sake. Concluded.

own; To Him our life and all be-long, To Him, and Him a-lone.

right we own;

## No. 107. Holy Spirit, Faithful Guide.

"I will guide thee with mine eye."—Psalm 32: 8.

M. M. WELLS. 1858.                    M. M. WELLS. by per.

1. Ho-ly Spir-it, faith-ful guide. Ev-er near the Chris-tian's side:

Gen-tly lead us by the hand. Pil-grims in a des-ert land;
D.S. Whisp'ring soft-ly, wan-der-er, come! Fol-low me. I'll guide thee home.

Wea-ry souls for e'er re-joice. While they hear that sweet-est voice

2 Ever present, truest Friend,
Ever near, Thine aid to lend,
Leave us not to doubt and fear,
Groping on in darkness drear.
When the storms are raging sore,
Hearts grow faint, and hopes give o'er,
Whispering softly, wanderer, come!
Follow me, I'll guide thee home.

3 When our days of toil shall cease,
Waiting still for sweet release,
Nothing left but heaven and prayer,
Wond'ring if our names were there;
Wading deep the dismal flood,
Pleading naught but Jesus' blood:
Whispering softly, wanderer, come!
Follow me, I'll guide thee home.

# No. 108. Seeking the Lost.

Written after hearing a sermon by J. H. Boyet, D. D., from James 5. 20.

A. J. B.                                                                    A. J. BUCHANAN.

1. Will you go and speak to the lost ones here? To the ones who have gone a-stray?
2. Will you go and speak to the sin - ners blind, And who walk in mid-night gloom?
3. Will you tell them all if they will be - lieve, That their souls will be truly blest?
4. Will you go and tell them the Sav - ior died, And pro-vi - ded for them the way?

Will you lead them back to the Shepherd's fold, From their wand'rings in sin's dark way?
Will you bear some light to their darken'd mind? Will you tell them their coming doom?
For the Sav - ior said that they shall re - ceive Precious blessings of peace and rest.
If they ful - ly trust in the Cru - ci - fied He will pardon their sins to - day.

CHORUS.

Will you seek............... them now, Will you
Will you seek them now, Will you seek them now? Will you

show............... them the way?
show them the way? Will you show them the way? Some one may be lost,

That you might lead home, To that bright land of per - fect day.

No. 109. Glorify His Name!

E. A. H.
Rev. Elisha A. Hoffman.

With animation.

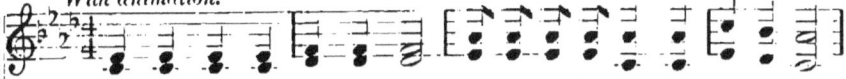

1. Praise the Lord who ran-somed you, Glo - ri - fy His name for - ev - er-more!
2. Oh, what bless-ings He be - stows! Glo - ri - fy His name for - ev - er-more!
3. Has He not been kind to you? Glo - ri - fy His name for - ev - er-more!
4. Was there ev - er love like this? Glo - ri - fy His name for - ev - er-more!
5. Let my tongue un - loos - ed be, Glo - ri - fy His name for - ev - er-more!

Faith - ful He has been and true, Glo - ri - fy His name for - ev - er - more!
How His grace from heav - en flows! Glo - ri - fy His name for - ev - er - more!
What more could your Sav - ior do? Glo - ri - fy His name for - ev - er - more!
Can the world be - stow such peace? Glo - ri - fy His name for - ev - er - more!
Let me through e - ter - ni - ty. Glo - ri - fy His name for - ev - er - more!

CHORUS.

Mag - ni - fy His name! Glo-ri - fy His name! Sing your al-le-lu - ias more and more!

Mag - ni - fy His name! Glo- ri - fy His name! Sing and praise the Lord forevermore!

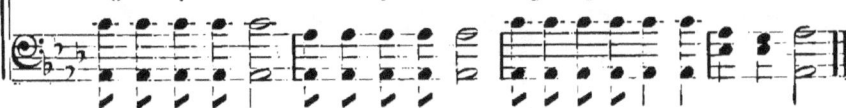

## No. 110. The Song of the Soul.

Rev. HENRY A. VON DULSEM.

T. C. O'KANE.

1. Oh, the song of the soul shall not die nor grow old, Nor lan-guish nor
2. In the beau - ti - ful land far a - way o'er the tide, The jas - per-walled
3. And the fair, gold - en harps in the hands of the blest, Shall thrill to a
4. And as a - ges fly on-ward, tho' worlds cease to be, And per - ish the

pine in the home of our King! But as a - ges fly onward new chords shall un-
home of the An - cient of Days, Where the ransomed ones shine as the sun in his
touch that no an - gel can give, As we sing in that land where the wea-ry shall
stars that in heav - en do throng, Still the joy of the soul shall be death-less and

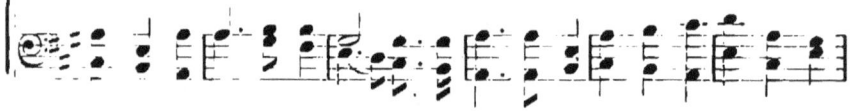

REFRAIN.

fold, New mel - o - dies meet-ing in-spire us to sing.
pride, Our long hal - le - lu - jahs of glo - ry we'll raise.
rest, Of One who hath died that a sin - ner might live.
free, And death-less and free the sweet notes of her song.

Oh, the song of the

soul! Oh, the song of the soul! For - ev - er in glo - ry the song of the soul!

# No. 111.     Let Him In.

Rev. J. B. Atchinson.

E. O. Excell.

1. There's a stranger at the door,   Let     Him in,
2. O - pen now to Him your heart,   Let     Him in,
3. Hear you now His lov - ing voice?   Let     Him in,
4. Now ad - mit the heav'n-ly Guest,   Let     Him in,

Let the Savior in,     let the Savior in,

He has been there oft be - fore,   Let     Him in;
If you wait He will de - part,   Let     Him in;
Now, oh, now make Him your choice,   Let     Him in;
He will make for you a feast,   Let     Him in;

Let the Savior in,     let the Savior in;

Let Him in ere He is gone, Let Him in, the Ho - ly One,
Let Him in, He is your Friend, He your soul will sure de - fend,
He is stand-ing at the door, Joy to you He will re - store,
He will speak your sins for - giv'n, And when earth ties all are riv'n,

Je - sus Christ, the Fa-ther's Son,   Let     Him in.
He will keep you to the end,   Let     Him in.
And His name you will a - dore,   Let     Him in.
He will take you home to heaven,   Let     Him in.

Let the Savior in,     let the Savior in.

# No. 112. I am Coming, Lord, to Thee.

W. A. O.　　"In returning, ye shall be saved," Isa. 30: 15.　　W. A. OGDEN.

*Earnestly.*

1. I am com-ing, Lord, to Thee, with a trem-bling heart, I am
2. I am com-ing, Lord, to Thee, with my load of sin, I am
3. I am com-ing, Lord, to Thee, but my faith is weak, I am

com-ing with my soul dis-trest; To Thy prom-ise now I fly,
com-ing, wea-ry, faint, and sore; Tho' I've slight-ed oft Thy grace,
com-ing, wilt Thou hear my cry? I have heard Thy gra-cious call,

Leave, oh, leave me not to die, I am com-ing, Lord, to Thee, for rest.
And have turned from Thee my face, I am com-ing, Lord, to roam no more.
At Thy lov-ing feet I fall, I am com-ing, tho' I faint and die.

CHORUS.

Com - ing, Lord, to Thee, Com - ing, Lord, to Thee;

I am com - ing,.... I am

Com - ing with my soul dis - trest, Com-ing, Lord, to Thee,

By permission.

## I am Coming, Lord, to Thee. Concluded.

com-ing,.....

com-ing, Lord, to Thee, I am com-ing, Lord, to Thee for rest.

## No. 113. Enough for Me.

E. A. H.

Rev. E. A. Hoffman.

1. O love sur-pass-ing knowl-edge! O grace so full and free!
2. O won-der-ful Sal-va-tion! From sin He makes me free!
3. O blood of Christ, so pre-cious, Poured out on Cal-va-ry!

FINE.

I know that Je-sus saves me, And that's e-nough for me.
I feel the sweet as-sur-ance, And that's e-nough for me.
I feel its cleans-ing pow-er, And that's e-nough for me.

D. S I know that Je-sus saves me, And that's e-nough for me!

REFRAIN.

D. S.

And that's e-nough for me! And that's e-nough for me!

# No. 114. My Mother's Hands.

Mrs. M. E. W.

Mrs. M. E. WILLSON,
Sister of the late P. P. BLISS.

*Slow and with great expression.*

1. Oh, those beautiful, beautiful hands! Tho' they neith-er were white nor small,
2. Oh, those beautiful, beautiful hands! How they cared for my in - fant days!
3. Oh, those beautiful, beautiful hands! As they pressed my ach - ing brow;
4. Oh, those beautiful, beautiful hands! Thin and wrinkled with age they grew;
5. Oh, those beautiful, beautiful hands! I stood by her cof-fin one day,
6. Oh, those beautiful, beautiful hands! I shall clasp them a - gain once more,

Yet my mother's hands were the fair - est, And love - li - est hands of all.
They guid-ed my feet in - to pleasant paths, And smoothed all the rug-ged ways.
They cooled the fev - er and eased the pain, Me-thinks I can feel them now.
But still they toiled on for the child so dear, And her love seemed more tender and true.
And I kissed those hands so cold and white, As qui - et and peaceful she lay.
As my feet touch the bank of the heav'nly land; We shall meet on that shin-ing shore.

CHORUS.

My mother's dear hands, her beautiful hands, Which guided me safe o'er life's sands,

I bless God's name for the mem - 'ry Of moth-er's own beau-ti - ful hands.

By permission.

# No. 115.   More Like Jesus.

Rev F. Merrick, D. D.                                T. C. O'Kane.

1. More like Jesus, more like Jesus would I be; More like Je-sus in sub-mis - sion,
2. More like Jesus, more like Jesus would I be; More like Je-sus, true and steadfast,
3. Blessed Jesus, come and make me all like Thee, All like Thee, O blessed Je - sus,

Like Him, trustful, un-re - pin - ing, Pa-tient like Him, like Him in hu-mil-i - ty.
Like Him striving, ev - er do - ing, Earn-est like Him, like Him in fi-del-i - ty.
In  the  glo - ry of Thy man-hood, In the beau-ty of Thy spot-less pur i - ty.

**CHORUS.**

More and more,     more and more,   More and more like Jesus ev-'ry day; ..
More and more,     more and more,   More like Jesus ev'ry day, ev'ry day;

More and more,     more and more,   More like Je-sus ev - 'ry day.
More and more,     more and more,

# No. 116.     Bring Them In.

ALEXCENAH THOMAS.

W. A. OGDEN.

1. Hark! 'tis the Shep-herd's voice I hear, Out in the des-ert
2. Who'll go and help this Shep-herd kind, Help Him the lit-tle
3. Out in the des-ert, hear their cry, Out on the mount-ain

dark and drear, Call - ing the lambs who've gone a - stray,
lambs to find? Who'll bring the lost ones to the fold,
wild and high, Hark! 'tis the Mas - ter speaks to thee:

CHORUS.

Far from the Shep-herd's fold a - way.
Where they'll be shel - tered from the cold? Bring them in,
"Go, find my lambs, where-e'er they be."

Bring them in, Bring them in from the fields of sin;

Bring them in, Bring them in, Bring the lit - tle ones to Je - sus.

By permission.

# No. 117.　　　He Leads Me On.

VICTORIA E. KEITH.　　　　　　　　　　　　　　　　　　　　W. A. OGDEN.

1. He leads me on thro' des - erts drear, And o - ver mountains wild;
2. He leads me where the tor-rents roar, And thro' the storm - y sea,
3. He leads me 'neath the star - ry sky, And thro' the noon-tide heat,
4. He leads me on my pil-grim way, By watch-ful care I'm bound,

Wher - e'er He leads me I'll not fear, For I am still His child.
I hear Him call - ing from the shore, "Fear not, but fol - low me."
I know He guides me with His eye, And stays my falt - 'ring feet.
There is no place a - long my way But that my God is found.

**REFRAIN.**

He leads me on, He leads me on, With Him my way is sure;

His heav'n-ly love en - fold - eth me, And keeps my heart se - cure.

Copyright, 1892, by W. A. Ogden. By per.

# No. 118.    When I See the Blood.

"When I see the blood I will pass over you. Ex." 12: 13.
"Christ our passover is sacrificed for us." 1 Chor. 5: 7.

JOHN.                             J. G. F.

1. Christ our Re-deem-er, died on the cross, Died for the sin-ner, paid all his due;
2. Chief-est of sin-ners, Je-sus can save, As He has prom-ised, so will He do;
3. Judg-ment is com-ing, all will be there, Who have re-ject-ed, who have refused?
4. Oh, what com-pas-sion, Oh, boundless love, Je-sus hath pow-er, Je-sus is true;

All who re-ceive Him, need nev-er fear, Yes, He will pass, will pass o-ver you.
Oh, sin-ner, hear Him, trust in His word, Then He will pass, will pass o-ver you.
Oh, sin-ner, hast-en, let Je-sus in, Then God will pass, will pass o-ver you.
All who be-lieve, are safe from the storm, Oh, He will pass, will pass o-ver you.

**CHORUS.**

When I see the blood, When I see the blood,
When I see the blood, When I see the blood,

*Rit.*

When I see the blood, I will pass, I will pass o-ver you.
When I see the blood, I will pass, I will pass o-ver you, o-ver you.

# No. 119. The Beautiful Pearly Gate.

A. J. B.

A. J. BUCHANAN.

1. Have you heard of that bright cit-y, With its o-pen pearl-y gates?
2. Have you heard of that bright riv-er, Clear as crys-tal pure and free?
3. Will you go to that bright cit-y, With im-mor-tals will you live?

Where the ran-somed ones are sing-ing, And the loved ones for us wait.
Flow-ing from the throne of glo-ry, Soon its beau-ties we shall see.
Trust in Je-sus, love and serve Him, And e-ter-nal life He'll give.

**CHORUS.**

O - - - ver there..... the an - - gels wait,.....
O - ver there, just o - ver there, the an-gels wait, the an-gels wait;

O - - - ver there,..... At the beau-ti-ful pearl-y gate.
O - ver there, just o - ver there,

# No. 120. Working and Waiting.

H. G. JACKSON, D. D.                                    Mrs. W. S. NICKLE.

1. Work-ing for the Mas-ter in the har-vest field, Paus-ing not for
2. Work-ing in the vine-yard, toil-ing for the Lord, Faith-ful-ly from
3. Wait-ing for the Mas-ter in the Bu - lah Land, Wait-ing till the
4. Wait-ing for the Mas-ter by the riv - er's side, Wait-ing, watching

wea - ri - ness or pain!  Joy - ful in His ser-vice, I the sic-kle wield,
dawn to set of sun;  Sweet will be the rest-ing, rich be my re-ward,
wel-come summons come,  Bid-ding me cross o - ver to the distant strand,
for the boatman pale,  Who will safe-ly bear me o'er the wa-ters wide,

CHORUS.

Gath'ring precious sheaves of gold - en grain.  Working,        working,
When to me my Lord shall say, "Well done."
There to dwell with Him in bliss at home.
To the peace-ful port with-in the veil.  Working, working, working, working,

Work - ing till the time of rest shall come;....  Wait - ing,
                                                   Wait - ing, wait-ing,

Copyright, 1892, by W. S. Nickle.

# Working and Waiting. Concluded.

wait - ing,
wait - ing, wait-ing,
Wait - ing  till  the Lord shall call  me home.

## No. 121.  All Hail the Power of Jesus' Name.

Rev. E. Perronet.    CORONATION.    O. Holden.

1. All  hail  the pow'r of  Je - sus' name! Let  an - gels pros-trate  fall;
2. Let  ev - 'ry kin-dred,  ev - 'ry tribe, On  this  ter - res-trial  ball,
3. Oh,  that with yon-der  sa-cred throng, We  at  His  feet may  fall;

Bring forth the roy - al  di - a - dem, And crown Him  Lord  of  all;
To  Him all  maj - es - ty  as-cribe, And crown Him  Lord  of  all;
We'll join the  ev - er - last - ing song, And crown Him  Lord  of  all;

Bring forth the roy - al  di - a - dem, And crown Him  Lord  of  all.
To  Him all  maj - es - ty  as-cribe, And crown Him  Lord  of  all.
We'll join the  ev - er - last - ing song, And crown Him  Lord  of  all.

# No. 122.  A Thousand Years!

H. BONAR.

M. L. McPHAIL.

1. Lift up your heads, de-spond-ing pilgrims; Give to the winds your needless fears:....
2. Tell the whole world these blessed tidings; Speak of the time of rest that nears:....
3. What if the clouds do for a mo-ment Hide the blue sky where morn ap-pears?....
4. Haste ye a-long, ye ages of glo-ry; Haste the glad time when Christ ap-pears;....

He who hath died on Cal-v'ry's mount-ain, Soon is to reign a thou-sand years.
Tell the op-pressed of ev-'ry na-tion, Ju-bi-lee lasts a thou-sand years.
Soon the glad sun of prom-ise giv-en Ris-es to shine a thou-sand years.
Oh! that I may be one found worth-y To reign with Him a thou-sand years.

CHORUS.

A thou-sand years!......... earth's coming glo - - ry, 'Tis the glad
A thousand years! earth's coming glo - ry, com-ing glo - ry,

day............. so long fore - told;.................... 'Tis the bright
'Tis the glad day so long fore - told, so long fore - told;

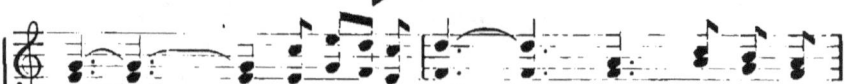

morn............. of Zi - on's glo - - ry Proph-ets fore-.
'Tis the bright morn of Zi - on's glo - ry, Zi - on's glo - ry

## A Thousand Years. Concluded.

saw........ ... ........ in times of old............ ...........
Proph-ets fore - saw in times of old, in times of old.

---

**No. 123.** **Revive Us Again.**

Dr. W. P. MACKAY.                                    English Melody.

1. We praise Thee, O God! for the Son of Thy love, For
2. We praise Thee, O God! for the Spir - it of light, Who has
3. All glo - ry and praise to the Lamb that was slain, Who has

CHORUS.

Je - sus who died, and is now gone a - bove. Hal - le - lu - jah!
shown us our Sav - ior, and scat tered our night. Hal - le - lu - jah!
borne all our sins, and has cleansed ev - 'ry stain. Hal - le - lu - jah!

Thine the glo - ry, Hal - le - lu - ja! A - men. Re - vive us a - gain.

4 All glory and praise to the God of all grace,
   Who has bought us, and sought us, and guided our ways.

5 Revive us again; fill each heart with Thy love;
   May each soul be rekindled with fire from above.

# No. 124.   I Long to Work for Thee.

Rev. William Fawcett, D. D.

W. S. Nickle

1. Je - sus, and may  I  work  for  Thee,  A  mor - tal  man  from
2. To  work  for  Thee,  the  Morn - ing  Star,  That  saw  me  lost,  and
3. To  work  for  Thee,  my  dear - est  Friend,  On  whom  my  ev - 'ry

sin  set  free?  A  mor - tal  man  with  short-'ning  days,  Per-
from  a  far  Shed  o'er  my  soul  a  light  di - vine,  And
hope  de - pends;  Who  washed  a - way  my  earth - ly  shame,  And

**CHORUS.**

mit - ted  thus  to  work  and  praise.  ⎫
com - fort - ed  this  heart  of  mine.  ⎬  I'll  work  for  Thee,  I'll
gave  to  me  a  new,  best  name.  ⎭

work  for  Thee,  Yes,  dear - est  Lord,  I'll  work  for  Thee.

4 Yes, blessed Jesus, yes, I may
Go work for Thee throughout this day,
And all the joy or good I crave,
Is but some fallen soul to save.

5 I'll work for Thee, Thou blessed One,
Eternal God, eternal Son,
And boast, but never boast in vain,
I'll work for Him who once was slain.

# No. 125.  Make Me a Worker for Jesus.

"And every man to his work." Mark. 13: 34.

EBEN. E. REXFORD.                                    T. C. O'KANE.

1. Make me a work-er for Je-sus, Steadfast and earn-est and true;
2. Let me be brave in the con-flict, Read-y to go where He needs,
3. Let me go out to the har-vest, Faith-ful-ly do-ing my part.
4. Make me a work-er for Je-sus, Trust-ing Him nev-er in vain,

Will-ing to work for the Mas-ter, What He would have me to do....
Sow-ing good seed for the har-vest, Pluck-ing up bri-ars and weeds.
Gath-er-ing sheaves for the gleaning, Stead-fast of pur-pose and heart.
Glad if I bind for the Mas-ter, Sheaves of God's beau-ti-ful grain.

**CHORUS.**

Make me a work-er for Je-sus, Hum-ble my la-bor may be, But

cheer-ful-ly done for the Mas-ter, Who hath done great things for me....

9

# No. 126. Come to Jesus Now.

H. G. JACKSON, D. D.                                                    VIOLA FROST MIXER.

1. Sin - ner, now the Spir - it warns you, Seek sal - va - tion while you may,
2. Heed the Gos - pel in - vi - ta - tion, Fly to Christ from sin and shame;
3. Long you've halt - ed, doubting, wav'ring, Half per-suad - ed to o - bey,
4. Wait no long - er, Je - sus calls you, Now de-cide for Him to live;
5. Just - i - fied by faith in Je - sus, All your doubts and fears will cease,

Now the door of mer - cy's o - pen, But there's dan-ger in de - lay.
Par - don now is of - fered free - ly, Free - ly of - fered in His name.
Long you've tar-ried at life's por - tals, O come in, come in to - day!
Come and prove His bound-less mer - cy, Prove how free - ly He'll for - give.
And your soul be - come God's tem - ple, Filled with light and love and peace

**REFRAIN.**

Come to Je - sus, Come to Je - sus, At His feet now hum-bly bow,

*Repeat. pp*

Oh, de - lay not, oh, de - lay not, But come, come to Je - sus now.

# No. 127. Where He Leads I'll Follow.

"Come unto Me, all ye that labor and are heavy laden, and I will give you rest." Matt. 11: 28.

W. A. O.                                                    W. A. OGDEN.

1. Sweet are the prom-is-es, Kind is the word; Dear-er far than
2. Sweet is the ten-der love Je-sus hath shown; Sweet-er far than
3. List to His lov-ing words. "Come un-to Me;" Wea-ry; heav-y-

an-y mes-sage man ev-er heard, Pure was the mind of Christ,
an-y love that mor-tals have known, Kind to the err-ing one,
lad-en, there is sweet rest for thee, Trust in His prom-is-es,

Sin-less I see; He the great ex-am-ple is, and pat-tern for me.
Faith-ful is He; He the great ex-am-ple is, and pat-tern for me.
Faith-ful and sure; Lean up-on the Sav-ior, and thy soul is se-cure.

CHORUS.

Where.................. He leads I'll fol - - - low,
Where He leads I'll fol-low, Where He leads I'll fol-low,

Fol - - - low all the way. Fol-low Jesus ev-'ry day.
Fol-low all the way, yes, fol-low all the way.

Copyright, 1885, by W. A. Ogden. By per.

# No. 128. Walking With the Savior.

" Ye ought so to walk, even as He walked." 1 John 2; 6.

Rev. M. Lowrie Hofford.

W. A. Ogden.

1. Are you walk-ing with the Sav - ior, In the true and liv - ing way?
2. Are you walk-ing with the Sav - ior, Are you dai - ly do - ing good?
3. Are you walk-ing with the Sav - ior, Does your heart with - in you burn,

**S:**

**FINE.**

Is the meek and low - ly Je - sus Your com - pan - ion ev - 'ry day?
Is your light a - round you burn-ing Just as bright-ly as it should?
While the sweetness of com - pas - sion From His lov - ing lips you learn?

**D. S.** Is the meek and low - ly Je - sus Your com - pan - ion ev - 'ry day?

Is your life that con - se - cra - tion To the cause of Him you love,
Are the poor in cot - tage low - ly, And the stran - ger by the way,
Do you wish that at the ev - 'ning, When the twi - light shad-ows fall,

Which would give you con - so - la - tion, Look-ing at it from a - bove?
Ev - er blest with words of kind-ness Which in love they've heard you say?
That the Sav - ior would be with you, And o - be-dient to your call?

**CHORUS.**

**D. S.**

Are you walk-ing with the Sav - ior, In the true and liv - ing way?

By per. of W. A. Ogden.

# No. 129. Sweetly Resting.

MARY D. JAMES.  W. WARREN BENTLEY.

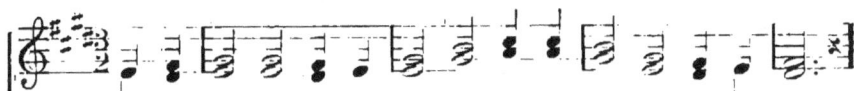

1. In the rift - ed Rock I'm rest - ing, Safe - ly shel-tered I a - bide:
2. Long pur-sued by sin and sa - tan, Wea - ry, sad, I long'd for rest;
3. Peace, which passeth un - der-stand-ing, Joy, the world can nev - er give,
4. In the rift - ed Rock I'll hide me, Till the storms of life are past,

There no foes nor storms mo-lest me, While with-in the cleft I hide.
Then I found this heav'nly shel - ter, O-pen'd in my Sav-ior's breast.
Now in Je - sus I am find - ing; In His smiles of love I live.
All se - cure in this blest ref - uge, Heed-ing not the fierc - est blast.

REFRAIN.

Now I'm rest - ing, sweet-ly rest - ing, In the cleft once made for me;

Je - sus, bless - ed Rock of A - ges, I will hide my - self in Thee.

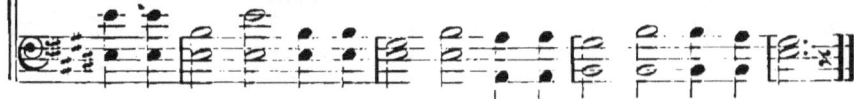

By permission.

# No. 130. Rest in the Lord.

IDA L. REED.

W. A. OGDEN.

1. Rest in the Lord and pa - tient - ly wait; Be - lieve on His word, His
2. Rest in the Lord and grieve not, nor fret; Thy works He'll re - ward, He
3. Rest in the Lord, He'll calm all Thy fears; He'll bear all thy bur - dens,

mer - cy is great; Rest in His love and fear not, for He, Tho'
can - not for - get; Rest in His love and fear not, for He, Tho'
dry all thy tears; Rest in His love and fear not, for He, Tho'

**CHORUS.**

dark be the hour, thy ref - uge shall be. Rest in the
dark be the hour, thy ref - uge shall be.
dark be the hour, thy ref - uge shall be. Rest in the Lord,

Lord, and pa - - tient-ly wait, Rest
Rest in the Lord, Pa-tient-ly wait, Patiently wait, Rest in the Lord,

*Rit.*

in the Lord, His mer - - cy is great.............
Rest in the Lord, His mer - cy is great, His mer - cy is great.

# No. 131. Entire Consecration.

FRANCES RIDLEY HAVERGAL. Chorus by W. J. K.
W. J. KIRKPATRICK.

1. Take my life, and let it be     Con - se - cra - ted, Lord, to Thee;
2. Take my feet, and let them be    Swift and beau - ti - ful for Thee;
3. Take my lips, and let them be    Filled with mes - sag - es for Thee;
4. Take my mo - ments and my days,  Let them flow in end - less praise;

Take my hands and let them move   At the im-pulse of Thy love.
Take my voice and let me sing     Al - ways, on - ly for my King.
Take my sil - ver and my gold.—   Not a mite would I with - hold.
Take my in - tel - lect, and use   Ev - 'ry pow'r as Thou shalt choose.

**CHORUS.**

{ Wash me in the Sav-ior's pre-cious blood, the precious blood, }
{ Cleanse me in its pu - ri - fy - ing flood, the heal-ing flood, }  Lord, I give to

Thee, my life and all, to be Thine, hence-forth, e - ter - nal - ly.

5 Take my will, and make it Thine;
  It shall be no longer mine;
  Take my heart,—it is Thine own,—
  It shall be Thy royal throne.

6 Take my love,—my Lord, I pour
  At Thy feet its treasure-store!
  Take myself, and I will be
  Ever, only, all for Thee.

By Permission.

# No. 132. He is Just the Same To-day.

Mrs. S. Z. KAUFMAN.     Heb. 13: 8.     I. N. McHOSE.

1. Have you ev - er heard the sto - ry of the Babe of Beth - le-
2. Have you ev - er heard how Je - sus walk'd up - on the roll - ing
3. Once while rest - ing on a pil - low in the ves - sel fast a-
4. Sure - ly you have heard how Je - sus prayed down in Geth - sem - a-

hem, Who was wor-shiped by the an - gels and by wise and ho - ly
sea, To His dear dis - ci - ples toss - ing on the waves of Gal - i-
sleep, There a - rose a might - y tem-pest on the wild and rag - ing
ne, How He shed His pre-cious life-blood on the rug - ged, shame-ful

men, How He taught the learn-ed doc - tors in the Tem-ple far a-
lee, How He res - cued sink-ing Pe - ter from his dan - ger and dis-
deep; "Peace, be still," the Lord com-mand-ed, ev - 'ry an - gry wave did
tree, Cru - el thorns His fore-head pierc-ing as His spir - it passed a-

way? I am glad to tell you, sin-ners, He is just the same to - day.
may? I am glad to tell you, sin-ners, He is just the same to - day.
stay; I am glad to tell you, sin-ners, He is just the same to - day.
way; Sin - ner, won't you come and love Him? He is just the same to - day.

# He is Just the Same To-day. Concluded.

CHORUS.

He's just the same to - day, Yes, just the same to - day, I'm

glad to tell you, sin - ners, He is just the same to - day.

## No. 133. Salvation's Free.

1. Come, ye that love the Lord, And let your joys be known;
2. Let those re - fuse to sing Who nev - er knew our God,

Cho.— I'm glad sal - va - tion's free, I'm glad sal - va - tion's free;

D. C. Chorus.

Join in a song with sweet ac - cord, While ye sur - round His throne.
But ser - vants of the heav'n-ly King May speak His grace a - broad.
Sal - va - tion's free for you and me; I'm glad sal - va - tion's free.

3. There we shall see His face,
And never, never sin;
There, from the rivers of His grace,
Drink endless pleasures in.

4. Then let our songs abound,
And every tear be dry;
We're marching thro' Immanuel's ground
To fairer worlds on high.

# No. 134.  God Will Help You Stand.

Words suggested by the following incident: A young man, the only son of respectable parents, well educated, and with natural qualities which would enable him to do a great deal of good in the world, became addicted to the use of strong drink. He tried in his own strength again and again to reform, but without success. Every effort seemed a failure. Finally, he determined to end his miserable existence by drowning in Lake Michigan. But by the providence of God, he was met on the way by a Christian gentleman, who persuaded him to abandon his purpose, and accept Jesus, which he did.

L. W. LYON.                                                                    P. BILHORN.

1. Tho' the way seems dark be - fore you, Broth - er, don't de - spair;
2. Is your heart de-pressed, my broth - er? Je - sus is your friend;
3. At the hearth-stone lov'd ones pray - ing, Plead - ing for their son,
4. Ma - ny pray'rs for you are ris - ing To the throne of grace,

Bright - er light shall yet shine o'er you, In this world of care.
He will save you, He will lead you To your jour - ney's end.
With a par - ent's sup - pli - ca - tion For the way - ward one.
Can you still His love de - spis - ing, Turn from Him your face?

He who by His might - y pow - er, Holds the sea and land,
Do not fear to trust Him, broth - er, See His wound - ed hand;
Loved one, cast your sins be - hind you, Join the ran - somed band;
Broth - er, rise from sin and sor - row, Take thy Fa - ther's hand;

Still is near, tho' dark the hour, He will help you stand.
He has died for your re - demp-tion, He will help you stand.
Grace suf - fi - cient He will give you, He will help you stand.
Fear no doubt of sin to - mor-row, He will help you stand.

# God Will Help You Stand. Concluded.

**CHORUS.**

He will help you stand. He will help you stand, He will help you stand,

Al - ways near, He'll not for - sake you, God will help you stand.

## No. 135. O For a Faith.

R. SIMPSON.

1. O for a faith that will not shrink, Tho' press'd by ev - 'ry foe,
2. That will not mur - mur nor com - plain, Be - neath the chast'n - ing rod,
3. A faith that shines more bright and clear When tem - pests rage with - out:
4. Lord, give us such a faith as this, And then, what-e'er may come,

That will not trem - ble on the brink Of an - y earth - ly woe!
But, in the hour of grief and pain, Will lean up - on its God;
That when in dan - ger knows no fear, In dark - ness feels no doubt;
We'll taste, e'en here, the hal-lowed bliss Of an e - ter - nal home.

# No. 136.  Yield Not to Temptation.

Words and Music by Dr. H. R. Palmer.

1. Yield not to temp-ta - tion, For yield-ing is sin, Each vic-t'ry will
2. Shun e - vil com - pan-ions, Bad language dis - dain, God's name hold in
3. To him that o'er-com - eth God giv - eth a crown; Thro' faith we shall

help you Some oth - er to win; Fight man - ful - ly on - ward,
rev - 'rence, Nor take it in vain; Be thoughtful and earn - est,
con - quer, Tho' oft - en cast down; He who is our Sav - ior,

Dark pas-sions sub - due, Look ev - er to Je - sus, He'll car-ry you through.
Kind-heart-ed and true, Look ev - er to Je - sus, He'll car-ry you through.
Our strength will re - new, Look ev - er to Je - sus, He'll car-ry you through.

**CHORUS.**

Ask the Sav - ior to help you, Com - fort, strengthen, and keep you;

He is will - ing to aid you, He will car - ry you through.

# No. 137.  Welcome for Me.

FANNY J. CROSBY.  WM. J. KIRKPATRICK.

1. Like a bird on the deep, far a-way from its nest, I had
2. I am safe in the ark; I have fold-ed my wings On the
3. I am safe in the ark, and I dread not the storm, Tho' a-

wan-der'd, my Sav-ior, from Thee; But Thy dear lov-ing voice call'd me
bo-som of mer-cy di-vine; I am fill'd with the light of Thy
round me the sur-ges may roll; I will look to the skies, where the

home to Thy breast, And I knew there was wel-come for me......
pres-ence so bright, And the joy that will ev-er be mine....
day nev-er dies, I will sing of the joy in my soul.....

CHORUS.

Wel-come for me, Sav-ior from Thee; A smile and a welcome for me;...

Now, like a dove, I rest in Thy love, And find a sweet ref-uge in Thee....
in Thee.

## No. 138.     Never to Say Farewell.

Rev. Elisha A. Hoffman.                                Ira Orwig Hoffman.

1. { We jour-ney to the home a-bove, Nev-er to say fare-well,
{ To yon fair pal - a - ces of love, [ Omit. . . . . . ] Nev-er to say fare-

2. { We'll meet our sainted parents there, Never to say farewell,
{ And heav'n with sisters, brothers share, [ Omit . . . . ] Nev-er to say fare.

well; Within that glo-rious summer land The ma - ny jewel'd mansions stand, And
well; Up - on the plains of per -fect light, Up-on the pavements golden bright, We'll

there'll we'll meet, at God's right hand, Nev-er to say farewell. Never to say fare - well,
walk with them, enrobed in white, Never to say farewell.

Nev-er to say farewell, Oh, we shall meet at God's right hand, Never to say farewell.

3 We'll meet beyond life's swelling flood,
   Never to say farewell,
Redeemed and washed in Jesus' blood,
   Never to say farewell:
Earth's long, long night will pass away,
Dissolving into heavenly day.
And we shall with our loved ones stay,
   Never to say farewell.

4 Oh, what a blessed hope is this,
   Never to say farewell!
What pure and perfect happiness,
   Never to say farewell!
Delivered from all sin and pain,
To reach yon fair, celestial plain,
And meet the loved and lost again,
   Never to say farewell.

* Very effective if unison parts are sung as a solo

# No. 139. Look and Live.

W. A. O.

W. A. OGDES.

1. I've a mes-sage from the Lord, Hal - le - lu - jah! The
2. I've a mes - sage full of love, Hal - le - lu - jah! A
3. Life is of - fered un - to thee, Hal - le - lu - jah! E-
4. I will tell you how I came; Hal - le - lu - jah! To

mes-sage un - to you I'll give, 'Tis re - cord-ed in His word,
mes-sage, oh! my friend for you, 'Tis a mes-sage from a - bove,
ter - nal life thy soul shall have. If you'll on - ly look to Him,
Je - sus, when He made me whole; 'Twas be - liev-ing on His name,

D. S.—'Tis re - cord-ed in His word,

*FINE.*

Hal - le - lu - jah! It is on - ly that you "look and live."
Hal - le - lu - jah! Je - sus said it, and I know 'tis true.
Hal - le - lu - jah! Look to Je - sus, who a - lone can save.
Hal - le - lu - jah! I..... trust-ed and He saved my soul.

*Hal - le - lu - jah! It is on - ly that you "look and live."*

**CHORUS.**
*D.S.*

"Look and live," .... my brother, live, Look to Je-sus now and live,
"Look and live," my brother, live, "Look and live,"

# No. 140. Sowing the Seed of the Kingdom.

F. A. F.

FRED. A. FILLMORE.

1. Are you sow-ing the seed of the king-dom, broth-er, In the morn-ing
2. Are you sow-ing the seed of the king-dom, broth-er, In the still and
3. Are you sow-ing the seed of the king-dom, broth-er, All a - long the

bright and fair? Are you sow-ing the seed of the king-dom, broth-er, In the
sol - emn night? Are you sow-ing the seed of the king-dom, broth-er, For a
fer - tile way? Are you get-ting read-y for the har-vest, brother, That will

CHORUS.

heat of the noon-day's glare? For the har - vest time is com-ing on,
har - vest pure and white?
come at the last great day? com-ing on,

And the reap-er's work will soon be done; Will your sheaves be
soon be done;

man-y, will you gar-ner an-y, For the gath'ring at the har-vest home?

# No. 141. The Half has Never Been Told.

FRANCES R. HAVERGAL.

R. E. HUDSON.

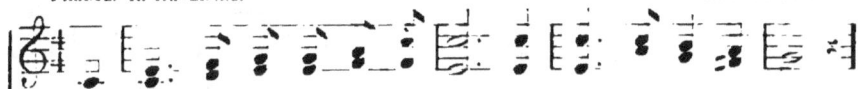

1. I know I love Thee bet - ter, Lord, Than an - y earth - ly joy,
2. I know that Thou art near - er still Than an - y earth - ly throng,
3. Thou hast put glad - ness in my heart: Then well may I be glad!
4. O Sav - ior, pre - cious Sav - ior mine! What will Thy pres - ence be,

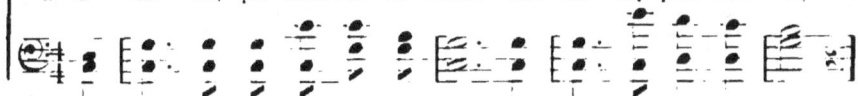

For Thou hast giv - en me the peace Which noth - ing can de - stroy.
And sweet - er is the thought of Thee Than an - y love - ly song.
With - out the se - cret of Thy love I could not but be sad.
If such a life of joy can crown Our walk on earth with Thee?

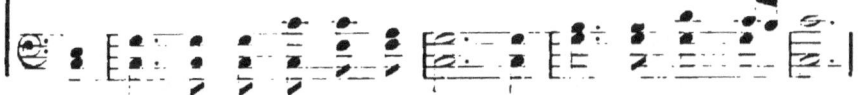

**CHORUS.**

The half has nev - er yet been told.
yet been told,
Of love so full and free;

The half has nev - er yet been told.
yet been told,
The blood—it cleanseth me.
cleanseth me.

*Rit.*

# No 142.  There Stood a Cross.

Rev. E. A. Hoffman.                                    Rev. J. H. Welch.

*Slow.*

1. On Cal - va - ry there stood a Cross, And nailed there-on was One
2. There the Re-deem - er gave His blood To ran - som me from sin,
3. Up - on that Cross, that bit - ter Cross, My weight of guilt He bore,
4. Be - fore' that Cross I weep and pray, And wor - ship and a - dore,

Who was the bear - er of my sin, God's well - be - lov - ed Son.
And made an end of all my guilt, And brought re - demp-tion in.
Se cured a clear-ance for my sins; My soul can ask no more.
And God's free grace I will ex - tol And laud for - ev - er - more.

**CHORUS.**

Oh, the blood of the Lamb! Oh, the blood of the Lamb,
That was shed on Cal - va - ry! It was shed for you,
It was shed for me, When He died up - on the tree.

# No. 143. He Saved Me, Hallelujah!

E. A. H.　　　　　　　　　　　　　　　　　　　Rev. Elisha A. Hoffman.

1. I earn-est-ly pray'd for de - liv-'rance from sin, And longed to be
2. My feet had been tread-ing the path-way of sin; My robes were de-
3. And now I'm re - joic - ing in Je - sus my King, And songs of thanks-

washed from de - file-ment with-in; To Je - sus for par-don and
filed and my spir - it un - clean; I went to the Sav - ior, the
giv - ing un - ceas-ing - ly sing; I praise and a - dore Him, the

cleans-ing I came, And He saved me, hal - le - lu - jah to His
dear Son of God, And He washed me and He cleansed me in His
dear Lamb of God, Who washed me and re-deemed me in His

won-der-ful name!
won-der-ful blood!
won-der-ful blood! He washed me, hal-le - lu-jah! He cleansed me, hal-le-

**Chorus.**

lu - jah! He saved me, hal - le - lu - jah to His won-der - ful name!

# No. 144.    Glory to God, Hallelujah!

FANNY J. CROSBY.                                               W. J. KIRKPATRICK.

1. We are nev - er, nev - er wea - ry of the grand old song;
2. We are lost a - mid the rap - ture of re - deem - ing love;
3. We are go - ing to a pal - ace that is built of gold;
4. There we'll shout re - deem-ing mer - cy in a glad, new song;

Glo - ry to God, hal - le - lu - jah! We can sing it loud as
Glo - ry to God, hal - le - lu - jah! We are ris - ing on its
Glo - ry to God, hal - le - lu - jah! Where the King in all His
Glo - ry to God, hal - le - lu - jah! There we'll sing the praise of

ev - er, with our faith more strong: Glo - ry to God, hal - le - lu - jah!
pin - ions to the hills a - bove: Glo - ry to God, hal - le - lu - jah!
splendor we shall soon be - hold: Glo - ry to God, hal - le - lu - jah!
Je - sus with the blood-wash'd throng: Glo - ry to God, hal - le - lu - jah!

**CHORUS.**

Oh, the chil-dren of the Lord have a right to shout and sing, For the

## Glory To God, Hallelujah! Concluded.

way is grow-ing bright and our souls are on the wing; We are go - ing by and
by to the pal - ace of a King! Glo - ry to God, hal - le - lu - jah!

## No. 145   I'm Believing and Receiving.

Arr. by W. J. K.

1. Sins of years are washed a - way, Black-est stains be - come as snow,
2. Doubts and fears are borne a - long, On the cur - rent's cease-less flow;
3. Ease and wealth be - come as dross. Worth-less, earth's de - light and show;

CHO.—*I'm be - liev - ing and re - ceiv - ing, While I to the fount - ain go,*

Dark-est night is changed to day, When I to the fount-ain go.
Sor - row chang - es in - to song, When I to the fount-ain go.
All my boast is in the cross, When I to the fount-ain go.

*And my heart the waves are cleansing Whit-er than the driv - en snow.*

4 Selfishness is lost in love,
   Love for Him whose love you know;
   All my treasure is above,
   When I to the fountain go.

5 Fighting is a great delight,
   Never will I fear the foe,
   Armed by King Jehovah's might,
   When I to the fountain go.

## No. 146.　It Will Never Grow Old.

Rev. W. W. Baily.

I. N. McHose.

1. O have you not heard of that coun-try a-bove, The name of its
2. That won-der-ful land has a cit-y of life, Ne'er darken'd with
3. A man-sion of won-der-ful beau-ty is there, And Je-sus that
4. They tell me its friend-ships and love are so pure, Its joys nev-er
5. In life's wea-ry con-flicts, there's fainting and care, Each year the gray

King and His in-fi-nite love? His chil-dren are death-less and
an-guish, nor dy-ing nor strife: Its tem-ples and streets are all
man-sion has gone to pre-pare: Its bright jas-per walls how I
die, and its treas-ures are sure; And loved ones de-part-ed, so
deep-ens a shade in the hair; But in the blest book where my

*D. S. It glad-dens my heart with a*

hap-py, I'm told; Oh, will it a-bide— will we nev-er grow old?
flash-ing with gold, Oh, can it be true, will we nev-er grow old?
long to be-hold, And join in the song that will nev-er grow old.
si-lent and cold, Will greet us a-gain where we'll nev-er grow old.
name is en-rolled, I read of that land where we'll nev-er grow old.

*joy that's un-told, To think of that land where we'll nev-er grow old.*

Chorus.

D. S.

'Twill always be new, it will nev-er de-cay; No night ever comes, it will always be day;

# No. 147.  Jesus, My All!

Rev. G. D. Watson, D. D.  Wm. J. Kirkpatrick.

1. My heart sings a song from morning till night: A song full of lib-er-ty, Love, and of light: A song of the Ca-naan-land, Hap-py and bright, And all of my *song* is Je-sus.

**Refrain.**

Je-sus. Je-sus. All of my song is Je-sus: From morning till night I sing with de-light.—Je-sus, my pre-cious Je-sus!

2 My heart hath a rest
  From sin and from fear:
A rest from all doubting.
  Disappointment and care:
A rest like the sky,
  Bending calm o'er the year,—
And all of my *rest* is Jesus.

3 My heart hath a gift,
  With value untold;
A gift of unbounded peace,
  Richer that gold:
A gift that the universe
  Can not all hold.—
And all of my *gift* is Jesus.

4 My heart hath a light
  In the cloudiest day:
A light which illumines
  Each moment my way:
A light which will not let
  The little one stray,—
And all of my *light* is Jesus.

5 My heart hath a Friend,
  All compassion and love,
Whose speech falls as soft
  As the star-light above:
A friend that abideth,
  And will not remove,—
And that dearest *friend* is Jesus.

6 My heart hath a home,
  And it wanders no more:
A home like to that
  On the glorified shore:
A home where all goodness
  Unbosoms its store,—
And all of my *home* is Jesus.

# No. 148.  We'll Never Say Good-by.

G. C. H.

GEO. C. HUGG.

1. In the morn of morns when we all meet there, In the home far a-
2. Nev-er sad-ness there, nei-ther grief nor tear, In that beau-ti-ful
3. With our kin-dred dear, in that home of love, While the a-ges e-

bove the sky, We'll re-call the scenes we have left be-hind, But we
home on high! But they swell the song, hap-py ran-som'd throng, And they
ter-nal fly, We will meet, and sing at the Sav-ior's feet, But we

**CHORUS**

nev-er will say "good-by." In the dawn - ing of the
In the dawn - ing clear of the

morn - ing, In that home far a-bove the sky; Hap-py
morn - ing fair,

meet - ing, hap-py greet - ing, When we nev-er say "good-by."
meet-ing there, hap-py greet-ing there,

# No. 149. Walk in the Light.

Bernard Barton.  Geo. C. Hugg. By per.

1. Walk in the light! so shalt thou know That fel - low - ship of love.
2. Walk in the light! and thou shalt find Thy heart made tru - ly His.
3. Walk in the light! and e'en the tomb No fear - ful shade shall wear;
4. Walk in the light! thy path shall be Peaceful, se - rene, and bright;

His spir - it on - ly can be - stow, Who reigns in light a - bove.
Who dwells in cloud-less light en - shrined, In whom no dark-ness is.
Glo - ry shall chase a - way its gloom, For Christ has conquered there.
For God by grace, shall dwell in thee, And God Him - self is light.

**CHORUS.**

Walk.......... in the light!................. Walk........ in the
Walk in the light, in the beau-ti - ful light of God! Walk in the light, in the

light!......... ............... Walk ............. in the
beau - ti - ful light of God! Walk in the light, in the

light!................. Walk in the beau - ti - ful light of God.
beau-ti-ful light of God!

## No. 150.　Happy in the Love of Jesus.

Henrietta E. Blair.　　　　　　　　　　　　　　　*Wm. J. Kirkpatrick.

1. Bright is the day-star shin-ing for me, Hap-py in the love of　Je - sus;
2. He　has re-deem'd me, I　am His own, Hap-py in the love of　Je - sus;
3. How　I am hon - or'd, how I am blest, Hap-py in the love of　Je - sus;
4. Firm　is my an - chor, steadfast and sure; Hap-py in the love of　Je - sus.

Now from my bondage grace makes me free, Hap-py in the love of　Je - sus.
Drawn by His mer - cy near to His throne, Hap-py in the love of　Je - sus.
Un - der His ban-ner sweet-ly I rest, Hap-py in the love of　Je - sus.
All things with pa-tience I can en-dure, Hap-py in the love of　Je - sus.

**Chorus.**

Praise from my full heart loudly shall ring, Born of the Spir-it, child of a King;

Heir to His glo - ry, now will I sing,—Happy in the love of　Je - sus.

Copyright, 1885, by Wm. J. Kirkpatrick. By per.

# No. 151. The Call for Reapers.

J. O. THOMPSON.                                                    J. B. O. CLEMM.

*Spirited.*

1. Far and near the fields are teem - ing With the waves of
2. Send them forth with morn's first beam - ing, Send them in the
3. O thou, whom thy Lord is send - ing, Gath - er now the

rip - ened grain; Far and near their gold is gleam - ing O'er the
noon-tide's glare; When the sun's last rays are gleam - ing, Bid them
sheaves of gold, Heav'nward then at ev'n - ing wend - ing Thou shalt

**CHORUS.**

sun - ny slope and plain. )
gath - er ev - 'ry - where. > Lord of har - vest, send forth
come with joy un - told. )

reap - ers! Hear us, Lord, to Thee we cry; Send them now the

sheaves to gath - er, Ere the har - vest time pass by.

# No. 152. Mercy is Boundless and Free.

HENRIETTA E. BLAIR.　　　　　　　　　　　　　　　W. J. KIRKPATRICK.

1. Thanks be to Je - sus, His mer - cy is free; Mer - cy is free,
2. Why on the mountains of sin wilt thou roam? Mer - cy is free,
3. Think of His good-ness, His pa - tience and love; Mer - cy is free,
4. Yes, there is par - don for all who be - lieve; Mer - cy is free;

REFRAIN. Je - sus, the Sav - ior, is look - ing for thee, Look-ing for thee,

mer - cy is free: Sin - ner, that mer - cy is flow - ing for thee,
mer - cy is free: Gen - tly the Spir - it is call - ing, "Come home,"
mer - cy is free: Plead-ing thy cause with His Fa - ther a - bove,
mer - cy is free: Come, and this mo - ment a bless - ing re - ceive,

look - ing for thee; Lov - ing - ly, ten - der - ly, call - ing for thee,

FINE.

mer - cy is bound-less and free.... If thou art will - ing on
mer - cy is bound-less and free.... Thou art in dark-ness, O
mer - cy is bound-less and free.... Come, and re - pent-ing, O
mer - cy is bound-less and free.... Je - sus is wait - ing, O

Call-ing and look - ing for thee....

Him to be - lieve, Mer - cy is free, mer-cy is free; Life ev - er-
come to the light, Mer - cy is free, mer-cy is free; Je - sus is
give Him thy heart, Mer - cy is free, mer-cy is free; Grieve Him no
bear Him pro - claim Mer - cy is free, mer-cy is free; Cling to His

# Mercy is Boundless and Free. Concluded.

*D. C. Refrain.*

last - ing thy soul may re - ceive, Mer - cy is bound-less and free....
wait - ing, He'll save you to - night, Mer - cy is bound-less and free....
long - er, but come as thou art, Mer - cy is bound-less and free....
mer - cy, be - lieve on His name, Mer - cy is bound-less and free....

## No. 153. A Sinner like Me!

C. J. B.     "Christ came into the world to save sinners."—1 Tim. 1: 15.     C. J. BUTLER.

*Slow.*

1. I was once far a - way from the Sav - ior, And as
2. I wan - der'd on in the dark - ness, Not a
3. And then, in that dark lone - ly hour,....... A

vile as a sin - ner could be; And I won - der'd if Christ the Re -
ray of light could I see; And the tho't fill'd my heart with
voice sweetly whis - pered to me, Say - ing, Christ the Re - deem - er has

*Rit.- - - - - -*

deem - er Could save a poor sin - ner like me.
sad - ness, There's no hope for a sin - ner like me.
power To save a poor sin - ner like me.

4 I listened: and lo! 'twas the Savior,
   That was speaking so kindly to me;
  I cried. "I'm the chief of sinners,
   Thou canst save a poor sinner like me!"
5 I then fully trusted in Jesus;
   And oh, what a joy came to me!
  My heart was filled with His praises,
   For saving a sinner like me.

6 No longer in darkness I'm walking,
   For the light is now shining on me;
  And now unto others I'm telling
   How He saved a poor sinner like me.
7 And when life's journey is over,
   And I the dear Savior shall see,
  I'll praise Him forever and ever,
   For saving a sinner like me.

## No. 154. He Came to Save Me.

HENRIETTA E. BLAIR.                                   WM. J. KIRKPATRICK.

1. When Je-sus 'laid His crown a-side, He came to save me; When
2. In my poor heart He deigns to dwell, He came to save me; O,
3. With gen-tle hand He leads me still, He came to save me; And
4. To Him my faith with rap-ture clings, He came to save me; To

on the cross He bled and died, He came to save me.
praise His name, I know it well, He came to save me. I'm so glad,
trust-ing Him I fear no ill, He came to save me.
Him my heart looks up and sings, He came to save me. I'm so glad,

I'm so glad, I'm so glad that Jesus came, And grace is free,
I'm so glad, I'm so glad that Jesus came, He (Omit........) came to save me.

## No. 155. Rock of Ages.

FINE.                                                      D. C.

1 Rock of Ages, cleft for me,
Let me hide myself in Thee;
Let the water and the blood,
From Thy wounded side which flowed,
Be of sin the double cure,
Save from wrath and make me pure.

2 Could my tears forever flow,
Could my zeal no languor know,
These for sin could not atone;

Thou must save, and Thou alone:
In my hands no price I bring,
Simply to Thy cross I cling.

3 While I draw this fleeting breath,
When my eyes shall close in death;
When I rise to worlds unknown,
And behold Thee on Thy throne,
Rock of Ages, cleft for me,
Let me hide myself in Thee.

# No. 156.  Satisfied.

HORATIUS BONAR.

GEO. C. HUGG.

1. When I a-wake in the sweet morn of morns, Af-ter whose dawning
2. When I shall meet with the ones I have lov'd, Clasp in my arms the
3. When I shall gaze on the dear face of Him, Who died for me, with

night ne'er re-turns: And with whose glo-ry the day ev-er burns.
long, long re-mov'd, And find how faith-ful the Lord then has prov'd,
eye no more dim, And praise Him ev-er with heav'n's swelling hymn,

**CHORUS.**

I shall be sat-is-fied; I shall be
I shall be sat-is-fied,

sat-is-fied; I shall be sat-is-fied;
I shall be sat-is-fied,

When in the like-ness of God I'm ar-rayed, I shall be sat-is-fied.

By permission.

# No. 157.  "Holy Spirit from Above."

Inscribed to Rev. C. H. Tyndall.

*Isaiah VI: 6 and 7.

Words and Music by H. R. PALMER, May, 1894.

MET. ♩ = 66.

1. Ho - ly Spir - it from a - bove, Fill our hearts with Thy pure love;
2. Take our sin - ful thoughts a-way; Lead, oh, lead us lest we stray;
3. With the al - tar's sa - cred Fire, Touch our lips, *our hearts in- spire:
4. Bless - ed source of Heav'n-ly light, Now dis - perse the gloom of night;

Oh, in - spire us with Thy zeal; May each soul Thy pres - ence feel.
Ho - ly Spir - it, faith - ful Guide, May each soul in Thee a - bide.
Oh, il - lume us by Thy grace; In each soul Thy im - age trace.
In our hearts for - ev - er shine; Fill each soul with joy di - vine.

REFRAIN.
f Don't hurry.

Ho - ly Spir - it from Thy throne a - bove, Fill us with the Sav-ior's dy - ing love;

Now descend upon us, Heav'nly Dove; Come Thou blessed Com fort - er. A - men.

# No. 158. My Jesus, I Love Thee.

A. J. GORDON. By per.

1. My Je - sus, I love Thee, I know Thou art mine;
2. I love Thee, be - cause Thou hast first lov - ed me,
3. I'll love Thee in life, I will love Thee in death,
4. In man - sions of glo - - ry and end - less de - light

For Thee all the fol - - lies of sin I re - sign;
And pur - chased my par - - don on Cal - va - ry's tree;
And praise Thee as long as Thou lend - est me breath;
I'll ev - er a - dore Thee in heav - en so bright;

My gra - cious Re - deem - er, my Sav - ior art Thou,
I love Thee for wear - ing the thorns on Thy brow;
And say when the death - dew lies cold on my brow,
I'll sing with the glit - ter - ing crown on my brow,

If ev - er I loved Thee, my Je - sus, 'tis now.

# No. 159.　Jesus Comes to Save.

Rev. A. J. Hough.　　　Acts. 2: 2.　　　J. E. Hall.

1. Floods of mer - cy break a-round us, Je - sus comes, comes to save!
2. While like rain our tears are fall - ing, Je - sus comes, comes to save!
3. Glo - rious light is dawn-ing o'er us, Je - sus comes, comes to save!
4. Hal - le - lu  jah! saints are sing-ing, Je - sus comes, comes to save!

Fet - ters fall that long have bound us, Je - sus comes, comes to save!
While these souls for help are call - ing, Je - sus comes, comes to save!
And the way grows bright be - fore us, Je - sus comes, comes to save!
Heav'n with joy - ous song is ring - ing, Je - sus comes, comes to save!

**CHORUS.**

Hal - le - lu - jah! joy - ful sto - ry, Je - sus comes, the King of glo - ry!

Hal - le - lu - jah! hal - le - lu - jah! Je - sus comes, comes to save.

## No. 160. Glory to His Name.

Rev. E. A. Hoffman.                                     Rev. J. H. Stockton.

1. Down at the cross where my Sav-ior died, Down where for cleansing from
2. I am so won-drous-ly saved from sin, Je - sus so sweet-ly a-
3. Oh, pre-cious fount - ain that saves from sin, I am so glad I have
4. Come to this fount - ain so rich and sweet; Cast thy poor soul at the

sin I cried; There to my heart was the blood ap - plied;
bides with - in; There at the cross where He took me in;
en - tered in; There Je - sus saves me and keeps me clean;
Sav - ior's feet; Plunge in to - day, and be made com - plete;

**Chorus**

Glo - ry to His name. Glo - ry to His name, Glo - ry to His name;

There to my heart was the blood ap - plied, Glo - ry to His name.

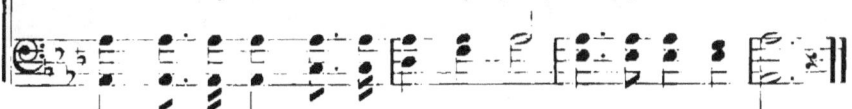

By permission.

# No. 161.　　　I'll Bear the Cross.

Mrs Harriet E. Jones.　　　　　　　　　　　　　　　　W. S. Nickle.

1. Al-though a thorn-y road I tread, I'll trust in Je - sus all the way.
2. Al-though the clouds ob-scure my sky, And sor-row's waves a-round me rise,
3. Al-though the thorns now pierce my feet, A - long a rough and drear-y road,

*Rit.*

A home of rest is just a - head, Where I will live with Him some day.
With Him who whis-pers, "It is I," I'll dwell some day, 'neath fair-er skies.
There is a rest and joy com- plete, In my Re-deem-er's bright a - bode.

CHORUS.

I'll jour-ney on be-neath the cross, Till Je - sus bids me lay it down;

*Rit.*

I'll shout and sing 'mid pain and loss, Till called where waits my fadeless crown.

# No. 162.     Our God is Marching On.

Tune: BATTLE HYMN OF THE REPUBLIC.

*Allegretto Maestoso.*

1. The light of truth is break-ing, On the mount-ain tops it gleams, Let it
2. From morning's ear-ly watch-es, Till the sett-ing of the sun, We will
3. We wield no car-nal weap-ons, And we hurl no fie-ry dart, But with

flash a-long the val-leys, Let it glit-ter on our streams, Till
nev-er flag nor fal-ter In the work we have be-gun, Till the
words of love and rea-son, We are sure to win the heart, And per-

all our land a-wak-ens, In its flush of gol-den beams; Our God is marching on.
forts have all sur-rend-ered And the vic-to-ry is won, Our God is marching on.
suade the poor transgressor To pre-fer the bet-ter part. Our God is marching on.

**CHORUS.**

Glo-ry, glo-ry, hal-le-lu-jah, Glo-ry, glo-ry, hal-le-lu-jah,

Glo-ry, glo-ry, hal-le-lu-jah, As we go march-ing on!......

# No. 163. Wandering Back.

A. M. HOOTMAN.

W. S. NICKLE

1. I am think-ing to - day of the scenes of my youth, And the
2. The old house, crib and barn, are re - placed by a new, And the
3. Yes, I'm glid - ing a - down the si - lent stream of time, And the

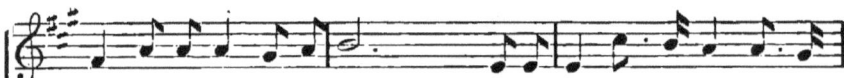

*p*

days that have long passed and gone;     Of the time when I played 'round my
home-stead seems strange to me now;      But my tho'ts wan-der back to my
ev - 'ning of life is at hand;            And their shadows seem to meet and gath-

dear moth - er's knee, When she sang me her lul - la - by song.
dear moth - er's side, Where in child-hood she oft kissed my brow.
er at my feet, Like the shells 'mid the bright drift-ing sand.

# Wandering Back. Concluded.

CHORUS.

No! the days will ne'er re-turn, when I was a boy, The

hopes of my youth fade a-way; I am journ'ying a-long

to the land of the blest, Where the scenes of my youth ne'er de-cay.

# No. 165.            All for Jesus.

"But Christ is all in all." Col. 3; 11.

Mrs. Mary D. James                                    Mrs. Joseph F. Knapp.

1. All     for Je - sus! all for  Je - sus! All   my be-ing's ran-somed pow'rs:
2. Let     my hands per-form His  bid - ding, Let  my feet run  in His  ways—
3. Since  my eyes were fixed on  Je - sus, I've  lost sight of all be - sides;
4. Oh,    what won-der! how a - maz-ing! Je - sus, glo-rious King of kings—

All   my thoughts,and words,and do - ings, All   my days,and all my hours.
Let   my eyes see  Je - sus on - ly, Let   my lips speak forth His praise.
So    en chained my spir - it's vis - ion, Look - ing  at  the Cru - ci - fied.
Deigns to  call  me  His be - lov - ed, Lets  me rest be-neath His wings!

REFRAIN.

All    for  Je - sus! all  for  Je - sus!  All  my  days, and  all  my hours.
All    for  Je - sus! all  for  Je - sus!  Let  my  lips speak forth His praise.
All    for  Je - sus! all  for  Je - sus!  Look - ing  at  the  Cru - ci - fied.
All    for  Je - sus! all  for  Je - sus!  Rest - ing now  be - neath His wings!

All  for  Je - sus! all  for  Je - sus!  All  my  days, and  all  my hours.
All  for  Je - sus! all  for  Je - sus!  Let  my  lips speak forth His praise.
All  for  Je - sus! all  for  Je - sus!  Look - ing  at  the  Cru - ci - fied.
All  for  Je - sus! all  for  Je - sus!  Rest - ing now  be - neath His wings!

By permission.

# No. 166.    Christ is All.

"Unto you therefore which believe he is precious." 1. Pet. 2: 7

*Effective as a Soprano Solo. Ad lib.*

W. A. WILLIAMS.

1. I en-tered once a home of care, For age and pen - u - ry were there,
2. I stood be-side a dy - ing bed, Where lay a child with ach-ing head,
3. I saw the mar-tyr at the stake, The flames could not his cour-age shake,
4. I saw the gos-pel her-ald go To Af - ric's sand and Green-land's snow,

Yet peace and joy with-al;   I asked the lone - ly moth - er whence
Wait-ing for Je - sus' call;   I marked his smile, 'twas sweet as May,
Nor death his soul ap - pall;   I asked him whence his strength was giv'n
To save from sa - tan's thrall;   Nor home nor life he count - ed dear,

Her help-less wid - ow - hood's de - fence,   She told me, "Christ was all."
And as his spir - it passed a - way,   He whispered, "Christ is all."
He look'd tri-umph - ant - ly to heav'n,   And an-swered, "Christ is all."
'Midst wants and per - ils owned no fear,   He felt that "Christ is all."

Christ is all, all in all,   She told me, "Christ was all."
Christ is all, all in all.   He whis-pered, "Christ is all."
Christ is all, all in all,   And an-swered, "Christ is all."
Christ is all, all in all,   He felt that "Christ is all."

5 I dreamed that hoary time had fled,
And earth and sea gave up their dead,
  A fire dissolved this ball;
I saw the Church's ransomed throng,
I heard the burden of their song,
  'Twas "Christ is all in all."
  Christ is all, all in all,
  'Twas "Christ is all in all."

6 Then come to Christ, oh! come to-day,
The Father, Son, and Spirit say;
  The Bride repeats the call;
For He will cleanse your guilty stains,
His love will soothe your weary pains,
  For "Christ is all in all."
  Christ is all, all in all,
  For "Christ is all in all."

From "Silver Tones." By per.

# No. 167.    We Shall Meet Again.

J. H. M.     To the memory of Mrs. Lillian Date Manny.     J. H. MANNY.

1. There is a sweet peace in be - liev - ing God's word, And
ful - ness of joy in His rest;.. And the pros - pect so pleas - ing for

D. S. And our loved ones have gone to that

FINE.

those who have heard Of the home in the realms of the blest There's a

beau - ti - ful home, They are free from all sor - row and pain.

D. S. to :S:

balm for the wea-ry, a rest near the throne, Where Jesus, the Savior, doth reign.

2 We'll be faithful and true to our calling below,
   Toil on in our labor of love,
Till our Master shall say at the close of the day,
   "Come, rest in my mansion above."
O how sweet it will be when from labor set free,
   To rest on the Savior's strong arm,
While He bears us safe o'er to the evergreen shore,
   Where no tempest or fear can alarm.

3 There the loved ones will meet on the golden-paved street,
   And with rapturous joy will behold   .
Our blessed Redeemer, whose presence so sweet
   Will anchor forever the soul.
O the joy of that rest in the realms of the blest,
   With the friends we have loved here below;
'Tis the theme of our song as we journey along,
   While His blessed salvation we know.

# No. 168.    I Will Sing of Jesus.

EDWARD A. BARNES.

Ps. 28: 7.

H. H. McGRANAHAN.

1. I will sing the love of Je - sus, Great - er love was nev - er known;
2. I will sing the words of Je - sus, Words of life from lips di - vine,
3. I will sing the grace of Je - sus, Which such won - ders will a - chieve,
4. I will sing the name of Je - sus, Hope of life that is to be;....

Yield-ing up... His life for sin - ners, Oh! what love to me was shown.
Full of com - fort, joy and cour-age, Pre-cious to... this soul of mine.
For by grace I claim re - demption, Since in Him I do be - lieve.
Sweet-er name was nev - er spok-en, Oh! how dear it is to me...

I will sing,     I will sing,     As my days are on the wing;
I will sing,     I will sing,

And my song... shall be of Je - sus, My Re-deem-er, and my King.

# No. 169. The Great Physician.

"Is there no balm in Gilead; is there no physician there?"—Jer. 8: 22.

Rev. Wm. Hunter, 1812.　　　　　　　　　　　　　Arr. by Rev. J. H. Stockton.

1. The great Phy - si - cian now is near, The sym - pa - thiz - ing
2. Your man - y sins are all for-giv'n, Oh, hear the voice of
3. All glo - ry to the dy - ing Lamb! I now be - lieve in
4. "The chil - dren too, both great and small, Who love the name of

Je - sus; He speaks the droop-ing heart to cheer, Oh, hear the voice of
Je - sus; Go on your way in peace to heav'n, And wear a crown with
Je - sus; I love the bless - ed Sav - ior's name, I love the name of
Je - sus, May now ac - cept the gra - cious call To work and live for

**CHORUS.**

Je - sus. "Sweet - est note in ser - aph song, Sweet - est name on

*Rit.*

mor-tal tongue, Sweetest car - ol ev - er sung, Je - sus, bless - ed Je - sus."

5 Come, brethren, help me sing His praise,
　Oh, praise the name of Jesus;
　Come, sisters, all your voices raise,
　Oh, bless the name of Jesus.

6 His name dispels my guilt and fear,
　No other name but Jesus:

　Oh, how my soul delights to hear
　　The precious name of Jesus.

7 And when to that bright world above,
　We rise to see our Jesus,
　We'll sing around the throne of love
　His name, the name of Jesus.

# No. 170.     Consecration.

Mrs. Mary D. James.       Mrs. Jos. F. Knapp.

1. My bod - y, soul, and spir - it, Je - sus, I give to Thee,
2. O Je - sus, might - y Sav - ior, I trust in Thy great name.
3. Oh, let the fire, de - scend - ing Just now up - on my soul,
4. I'm Thine, O bless - ed Je - sus, Wash'd by Thy pre - cious blood,

A con - se - crat - ed off - 'ring, Thine ev - er - more to be.
I look for Thy sal - va - tion, Thy prom - ise now I claim.
Con - sume my hum - ble off - 'ring, And cleanse and make me whole.
Now seal me by Thy Spir - it, A sac - ri - fice to God.

REFRAIN.

My all is on the al - tar, I'm wait - ing for the fire;

*Rit.*

Wait - ing, wait - ing, wait - ing, I'm wait - ing for the fire.

From "Notes of Joy." By Per.

# No. 171. At the Cross.

R. E. Hudson.

1. A - las! and did my Sav - ior bleed, And did my Sovereign die,
2. Was it for crimes that I have done, He groaned up - on the tree?
3. But drops of grief can ne'er re - pay The debt of love I owe;

Would He de - vote that sa - cred head For such a worm as I?
A - maz - ing pit - y, grace un-known, And love be - yond de - gree!
Here, Lord, I give my - self a - way, 'Tis all that I can do!

CHORUS.

At the cross, at the cross, where I first saw the light, And the

bur-den of my heart rolled a - way—
rolled a-way,
It was there by faith

I re - ceived my sight, And now I am hap - py all the day.

## No. 172. Have You Been to the Fountain?

C. A. S.                                                                    C. A. SHAW.

1. Have you been to the fount-ain for the cleans-ing from sin? Are you
2. Does the love, bound-less love of Je-sus dwell in your soul? Are you
3. Are you now ful-ly trust-ing in the love of the Lord? Are you

washed        in the blood?     Have you found full sal-va-tion by the
washed        in the blood?     Have you faith's full assurance as you
washed        in the blood?     Are your hopes firmly anchored in the

Are you washed        in the blood?

cleans-ing with-in?  Are you washed        in the blood?     Are your
near heav-en's goal, That you're washed        in the blood?
truth of His word? Are you washed        in the blood?

Are you washed        in the blood?

**CHORUS.**

gar  -  ments pure and white? Are they washed     in the blood?   Are you
Are your gar-ments pure and white?   Are they washed     in the blood?

walk - - ing in the light?   Are you walking in the light of  God?
Are you walk - ing in the light,     walking in the light of  God?

Copyright, 1892, by C. A. Shaw. By per.

# No. 173.　　God be With You!

J. E. RANKIN, D. D.　　　　　　　　　　　　　　　W. G. TOMER.

1. God be with you till we meet a - gain!— By His counsels guide, up-
2. God be with you till we meet a - gain!—'Neath His wings pro-tect-ing
3. God be with you till we meet a - gain!—When life's per - ils thick con-
4. God be with you till we meet a - gain!—Keep love's ban-ner float-ing

hold you, With His sheep se - cure - ly fold you; God be
hide you, Dai - ly man - na still di -vide you; God be
found you, Put His arms un - fail - ing round you; God be
o'er you, Smite death's threat'ning wave be - fore you; God be

**CHORUS.**

with you till we meet a - gain! Till we meet!.......... Till we
　　　　　　　　　　　　　　　　　　　　Till we meet! Till we

meet! Till we meet at Je - sus' feet; Till we
meet a - gain!　　　　　　　　　　Till we meet!

meet!....... Till we meet! God be with you till we meet a - gain!
Till we meet! Till we meet Till we meet.

# No. 174. The Happy Pilgrim.

ANON.

1. { I saw a hap-py pil-grim, In shin-ing gar-ments glad,
   { His back did bear no bur-den— He'd laid it at the cross—
2. { The Sum-mer sun was shin-ing, But He had found a shield—
   { His soul was filled with glo-ry As He kept press-ing on;

Trav - el - ing up the mount-ain, It seemed that he was glad: )
The blood of Christ, his Sav - ior, Had cleans'd him from all dross. )
A co-vert in the des - ert— Up - on life's bat - tle - field; )
He heard no oth - er mu - sic But what was heav - en - born. )

REFRAIN.

Then palms of Vic - to - ry, crowns of Glo-ry, Palms of Vic - to - ry we shall wear.

3 No pleasure in sin's arbor
  Could catch his eye or ear,
The precious name of Jesus
  Was all he loved to hear.
Thus he kept pressing onward,
  Delighted with the way,
And shouting, Glory! Glory!
  To Jesus all the day.

4 I saw him in the morning,
  On Canaan's sunny plain
Gathering for the Master
  The rich and golden grain;
He bound them up in bundles
  Until the angels come,
To gather in the harvest
  In heaven, his happy home.

5 I saw him in midsummer,
  Still happy on the way,
He'd reach the land of Beulah,
  Where birds sing night and day;
He found a store of honey,
  And wine upon the lees,
And fruit in rich abundance
  Upon life's living trees.

6 I saw him in the evening,
  Life's sun was bending low,
He'd reached the Golden City,—
  His robes still white as snow:
He joined the bridal cortege,
  And drank of the new wine,
And now among the angels,
  Eternally doth shine.

# No. 175.  Only Trust Him.

*"Take my yoke upon you, and learn of me: and ye shall find rest unto your souls."—Matt. 11: 29.*

Rev. J. H. S.                                              Rev. J. H. Stockton.

1. Come, ev - 'ry soul by sin oppress'd. There's mer - cy with the Lord,
2. For Je - sus shed His pre - cious blood Rich bless-ings to be - stow;
3. Yes. Je - sus is the Truth. the Way. That leads you in - to rest;
4. Come then, and join this ho - ly band. And on to glo - ry go,

And He will sure - ly give you rest, By trust - ing in His word.
Plunge now in - to the crim - son flood That wash - es white as snow.
Be - lieve in Him with - out de - lay, And you are ful - ly blest.
To dwell in that ce - les - tial land. Where joys im - mor - tal flow.

CHORUS.

On - ly trust Him, on - ly trust Him, On - ly trust Him now;

He will save you, He will save you, He will save you now.

By permission.

# No. 176. Kind Words Can Never Die.

A. H.

ABBY HUTCHINSON

1. Kind words can nev-er die, Cher-ish'd and blest, God knows how deep they lie,
2. Sweet tho'ts can nev-er die, Tho', like the flow'rs, Their brightest hues may fly
3. Our souls can nev-er die, Tho' in the tomb We may all have to lie,

Stored in the breast: Like childhood's simple rhymes, Said o'er a thou-sand times
In win-try hours, But when the gen-tle dew Gives them their charms a-new,
Wrapped in its gloom. What tho' the flesh de-cay, Souls pass in peace a-way,

Ay, in all years and climes, Dis-tant and near. Kind words can nev-er die.
With ma-ny an ad-ded hue They bloom a-gain. Sweet tho'ts can nev-er die.
Live thro' e-ter-nal day With Christ a-bove. Our souls can nev-er die,

*Rit. . . .*

Nev-er die, nev-er die, Kind words can nev-er die, No, nev-er die.
Nev-er die, nev-er die, Sweet tho'ts can nev-er die, No, nev-er die.
Nev-er die, nev-er die, Our souls can nev-er die, No, nev-er die.

## No. 177. A Band of Brethren.

Respectfully dedicated to the Chicago Praying Band.

L. H.

1. Oh, we're a band of brethren dear, I be-long to this band, hal-le-lu jah!
   Who live as pilgrim strangers here, I be-long to this band, hal-le-lu-jah!

2. The Prophets, and A-pos-tles, too, Did be-long to this band, hal-le-lu-jah!
   And all God's children here be-low Do be-long to this band, hal-le lu-jah!

REFRAIN.

Hal-le-lu - jah! hal-le-lu - jah! I be-long to this band, hal-le-lu-jah!

3 King David on his throne of state,
  Did belong to this band, hallelujah!
  And Lazarus at the rich man's gate,
  Did belong to this band, hallelujah!

4 I hope to meet my brethren there,
  They belong to this band, hallelujah!
  Who often joined with me in prayer,
  They belonged to this band, hallelujah!

## No. 178. Refining Fire.

1. Re - fin - ing fire, go through my heart, Re - fin - ing fire go through my heart,
2. Scat-ter Thy life through ev-'ry part, Scat-ter Thy life thro' ev - 'ry part,
3. O that it now from heav'n might fall, O that it now from heav'n might fall,
4. Come, Ho-ly Ghost, for Thee I call, Come, Ho-ly Ghost, for Thee I call,
REF. We're kneeling at the mer-cy seat, We're kneeling at the mer-cy seat,

Re - fin - ing fire, go thro' my heart, Il - lu - min - ate my soul.....
Scat - ter Thy life thro' ev - 'ry part, And sanc-ti - fy the whole.
O that it now from heav'n might fall, And all my sins con - sume....
Come, Ho - ly Ghost, for Thee I call, Spir - it of burn - ing, come...
We're kneeling at the mer - cy seat, Where Je - sus an-swers prayer.

## No. 179. Duane Street.

1. He dies! the friend of sin - ners dies! Lo! Sa - lem's daugh-ters weep a - round; A sol-emn darkness veils the skies. A sud - den trembling shakes the ground. Come, saints, and drop a tear or two For

*D. S.* *Him who groan'd be-neath your load; He shed a thousand drops for you.—A thousand drops of rich - er blood.*

2 Here's love and grief beyond degree,
The Lord of glory dies for man!
But lo! what sudden joys we see,
Jesus, the dead, revives again!
The rising God forsakes the tomb;
In vain the tomb forbids His rise;
Cherubic legions guard Him home,
And shout Him welcome to the skies.

3 Break off your tears, ye saints, and tell
How high your great Deliverer reigns;
Sing how He spoiled the hosts of hell,
And led the monster Death in chains.
Say, "Live forever, wondrous King!
Born to redeem, and strong to save;"
Then ask the monster, "Where's thy sting?"
And, "Where's thy victory boasting grave?"

### No. 180. Come, Holy Spirit,
#### Sing to tune BELERMA—135.

1 Come, Holy Spirit, heavenly Dove,
With all Thy quick'ning powers;
Kindle a flame of sacred love
In these cold hearts of ours.

2 Father, and shall we ever live
At this poor dying rate—
Our love so faint, so cold to Thee,
And Thine to us so great?

3 Come, Holy Spirit, heavenly Dove,
With all Thy quick'ning powers;
Come, shed abroad a Savior's love,
And that shall kindle ours.

### No. 181. Oh, for a Closer Walk
#### Sing to tune BELERMA—135.

1 Oh, for a closer walk with God,
A calm and heavenly frame;
A light to shine upon the road
That leads me to the Lamb.

2 The dearest idol I have known,
Whate'er that idol be,
Help me to tear it from Thy Throne,
And worship only Thee.

3 So shall my walk be close with God,
Calm and serene my frame;
So purer light shall mark the road
That leads me to the Lamb.

## No. 182. I'm a Pilgrim.

Mrs. M. S. B. Dana.

1. I'm a pil-grim, and I'm a stran-ger; I can tar - ry, I can
2. There the glo - ry is ev - er shin - ing; O my long-ing heart, my
3. There's the cit - y to which I jour - ney; My Re-deem - er, my Re-

D.C. I'm a pil-grim, and I'm a stran - ger; I can tar - ry, I can

FINE.

tar - ry but a night; Do not de - tain me, for I am
long - ing heart is there; Here in this coun - try so dark and
deem - er is its light, There is no sor - row nor an - y

tar - ry but a night.

D. C.

go - ing To where the fount - ains are ev - er flow - ing.
drear - y, I long have wan - dered for - lorn and wea - ry.
sigh - ing, Nor an - y tears there, nor an - y dy - ing.

## No. 183. Come to Jesus.

English.

1. Come to Je - sus, come to Je - sus, Come to Je - sus, just now, Just now, come to

Je - sus, come to Je - sus, just now.

2 He will save you.
3 Oh, believe Him.
4 He is able.
5 He is willing.
6 He'll receive you.
7 Call upon Him.
8 He will hear you.
9 Look unto Him.
10 He'll forgive you.
11 Flee to Jesus,
12 He will cleanse you.
13 He will clothe you.
14 Jesus loves you.
15 Don't reject Him.
16 Only trust Him.
17 Hallelujah, Amen.

## No. 184.    Rest for the Weary.

Rev. W. McDonald.

1. In the Christian's home in glo - ry, There re - mains a land of
2. He is fit - ting up my man - sion, Which e - ter - nal - ly shall
3. Sing, oh, sing, ye heirs of glo - ry; Shout your tri - umph as you

rest, There my Sav - ior's gone be - fore me, To ful - fill my soul's re - quest.
stand, For my stay shall not be tran - sient In that ho - ly, hap - py land.
go; Zi - on's gate will o - pen for you, You shall find an entrance through.

CHORUS.

{ There is rest for the wea - ry, There is rest for the wea - ry,
{ On the oth - er side of Jor - dan, In the sweet fields of E - den,

There is rest for the wea - ry, There is rest for you. }
Where the tree of life is bloom - ing, There is rest for you. }

## No. 185.   Blest be the Tie.

1 Blest be the tie that binds
  Our hearts in Christian love;
  The fellowship of kindred minds
  Is like to that above.

2 Before our Father's throne,
  We pour our ardent pray'rs;

Our fears, our hopes, our aims are one,
  Our comforts and our cares.

3 We share our mutual woes;
  Our mutual burdens bear;
  And often for each other flows
  The sympathizing tear.

4 When we asunder part,
  It gives us inward pain;
  But we shall still be joined in heart,
  And hope to meet again.

# No. 186. I'm Going Home to Die no More.

WM HUNTER, D. D.  Arranged by Rev. WM. McDONALD

1. { My heav'n-ly home is bright and fair; Nor pain, nor death can en - ter there: }
{ It's glitt'ring tow'rs the sun outshines; That heav'nly man-sion shall be mine. }

Cho. { I'm go - ing home, I'm go - ing home, I'm go - ing home to die no more! }
{ To die no more, to die no more, I'm go - ing home to die no more! }

2 My Father's house is built on high,
Far, far above the starry sky:
When from this earthly prison free,
That heavenly mansion mine shall be.

3 While here a stranger far from home,
Affliction's waves may 'round me foam;
Although like Lazarus, sick and poor,
My heavenly mansion is secure.

4 Let others seek a home below,
Which flames devour, or waves o'erflow;
Be mine a happier lot to own,
A heavenly mansion near the throne.

5 Then fail this earth, let stars decline
And sun and moon refuse to shine,
All nature sink and cease to be,
That heavenly mansion stands for me.

## No. 187. I Believe Jesus Saves.

Tune—"Sweet by and by."

Key of G.

1 I am coming to Jesus for rest,
Rest, such as the purified know;
My soul is athirst to be blest,
To be washed and made whiter than snow.

CHORUS.
I believe Jesus saves,
And His blood washes whiter than snow;
I believe Jesus saves,
And His blood washes whiter than snow.

2 In coming, my sin I deplore,
My weakness and poverty show;
I long to be saved evermore,
To be washed and made whiter than snow.

3 To Jesus I give up my all,
Every treasure and idol I know;
For His fullness of blessing I call,
Till His blood washes whiter than snow.

4 I am trusting in Jesus alone,
Trusting now His salvation to know;
And His blood doth fully atone,
I am washed and made whiter than snow.

5 My heart is in raptures of love,
Love, such as the ransomed ones know;
I am strengthened with might from above;
I am washed and made whiter than snow.

## No. 188. Nearer, my God, to Thee.

1 Nearer, my God, to Thee!
Nearer to Thee,
E'en though it be a cross
That raiseth me;
Still all my song shall be,
Nearer, my God, to Thee,
Nearer to Thee!

2 Though like a wanderer,
The sun gone down,
Darkness be over me,
My rest a stone;
Yet in my dreams I'd be
Nearer, my God, to Thee,
Nearer to Thee!

3 There let the way appear,
Steps unto heaven;
All that Thou sendest me,
In mercy given;
Angels to beckon me
Nearer, my God, to Thee,
Nearer to Thee!

4 Then, with my waking thoughts
Bright with Thy praise,
Out of my stony griefs
Bethel I'll raise;
So by my woes to be
Nearer, my God, to Thee,
Nearer to Thee!

## No. 189. My Country, 'tis of Thee.

S. F. Smith.  (AMERICA. 6s, 4s.)

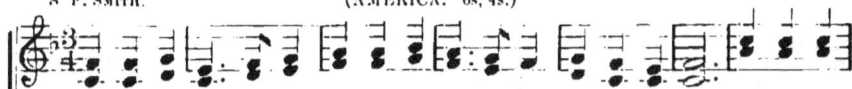

1. My coun-try, 'tis of thee, Sweet land of lib-er-ty, Of thee I sing; Land where my
2. My na-tive coun-try, thee, Land of the no-ble free, Thy name I love; I love thy
3. Let mu-sic swell the breeze, And ring from all the trees Sweet freedom's song; Let mortal
4. Our fa-ther's God, to Thee, Au-thor of lib-er-ty, To Thee we sing; Long may our

*Cres.*

fa-thers died, Land of the Pilgrim's pride, From ev'ry mountain side, Let freedom ring.
rocks and rills, Thy woods and templed hills, My heart with rapture thrills, Like that above.
tongues awake, Let all that breathe partake, Let rocks their silence break, The sound prolong.
land be bright, With freedom's holy light, Pro-tect us by Thy might, Great God, our King!

## No. 190. Marching to Glory.

Tune—"Marching Through Georgia."

Key of B Flat.

1 Come with hearts and voices now and sing
a gospel song,
Sing it with a spirit that will move the
mighty throng:
Sing it till the world shall hear the echoes
loud and long,
While we are marching to glory.

CHORUS.—

Then hail! all hail! the coming jubilee!
Redeemed from sin, our Jesus makes us
free;
Now we'll shout salvation over mountain,
land and sea,
While we are marching to glory!

2 Gird the gospel armor on and duty's call
obey;
See the host of Satan ready marshalled for
the fray:
Going forth to meet them we will watch
and fight and pray,
While we are marching to glory

3 Forward then to battle, 'neath the banner
of the cross;
Counting worldly honors at their best as
only dross;
Jesus is our Captain, and we ne'er can
suffer loss,
While we are marching to glory!

## No. 191. Oh, how Happy are They.

Tune—"Tramp, Tramp."

Key of A Flat.

1 Oh, how happy are they
Who the Savior obey,
And have laid up their treasures above;
Tongue can never express
The sweet comfort and peace
Of a soul in its earliest love.

CHORUS.

We'll all shout hallelujah
As we march along the way,
And we'll sing our Savior's love
With the shining host above,
And with Jesus we'll be happy all the day.

2 That sweet comfort was mine,
When the favor divine
I received through the blood of the Lamb:
When my heart first believed,
What a joy I received—
What a heaven in Jesus' name!

3 'Tis a heaven below
My Redeemer to know,
And the angels can do nothing more
Than to fall at His feet,
And the story repeat,
And the lover of sinners adore.

4 Jesus all the day long
Is my joy and my song,
Oh! that all His salvation might see!
He hath cleansed me, I cried;
And I'm now sanctified,
Oh, exalt and adore Him with me.

## No. 192.     Oh, How I Love Jesus.

JOHN NEWTON.

[*Omit in Repeat........*]

CHORUS.

[*Omit in Repeat........*]

1 How sweet the name of Jesus sounds
   In a believer's ear,
It soothes his sorrows, heals his wounds,
   And drives away his fear.

Cho.—‖:Oh, how I love Jesus!:‖
   Because He first loved me:
‖:How can I forget Thee?:‖
   Dear Lord, remember me.

2 It makes the wounded spirit whole,
   And calms the troubled breast;
'T is manna to the hungry soul,
   And to the weary rest.

3 I would Thy boundless love proclaim
   With every fleeting breath;
So shall the music of Thy name
   Refresh my soul in death.

## Lenox.

### No. 193.    Arise my Soul.

1 Arise, my soul, arise;
   Shake off thy guilty fears;
The bleeding Sacrifice
   In my behalf appears:
‖: Before the throne my Surety stands, :‖
My name is written on His hands.

2 He ever lives above,
   For me to intercede;
His all-redeeming love,
   His precious blood, to plead;
‖: His blood atoned for all our race, :‖
And sprinkles now the throne of grace.

3 Five bleeding wounds He bears,
   Received on Calvary;
They pour effectual prayers,
   They strongly plead for me:
‖: "Forgive him, O forgive," they cry, :‖
"Nor let that ransomed sinner die."

4 The Father hears Him pray,
   His dear anointed One:
He can not turn away
   The presence of His Son.
: His Spirit answers to the blood, :‖
And tells me I am born of God.

5 My God is reconciled;
   His pardoning voice I hear:
He owns me for His child;
   I can no longer fear:
‖: With confidence I now draw nigh, :‖
And, "Father, Abba, Father," cry.

### No 194.    Blow ye the Trumpet

1 Blow ye the trumpet, blow,
   The gladly solemn sound;
Let all the nations know,
   To earth's remotest bound,
‖: The year of jubilee is come: :‖
Return, ye ransom'd sinners, home.

2 Jesus, our great High Priest,
   Hath full atonement made;
Ye weary spirits, rest;
   Ye mournful souls, be glad:
‖: The year of jubilee is come, :‖
Return, ye ransomed sinners, home.

3 Extol the Lamb of God,
   The all-atoning Lamb;
Redemption in His blood
   Throughout the world proclaim:
‖: The year of jubilee is come! :‖
Return, ye ransomed sinners, home.

4 Ye slaves of sin and hell,
   Your liberty receive,
And safe in Jesus dwell,
   And blest in Jesus live:
‖: The year of jubilee is come!
Return, ye ransomed sinners, home.

5 Ye who have sold for naught
   Your heritage above,
Shall have it back unbought,
   The gift of Jesus' love:
‖: The year of jubilee is come! :‖
Return, ye ransomed sinners, home.

## No. 195. The Home Over There.

1. Oh, think of the home over there,
   By the side of the river of light,
   Where the saints, all immortal and fair,
   Are robed in their garments of white.

REF.—Over there, over there,
   Oh, think of the home over there.

2 Oh, think of the friends over there,
   Who before us the journey have trod,
   Of the songs that they breathe on the air,
   In their home in the palace of God.

REF.—Over there, over there,
   Oh, think of the friends over there.

3 My Savior is now over there,
   There my kindred and friends are at rest;
   Then away from my sorrow and care,
   Let me fly to the land of the blest.

REF.—Over there, over there,
   My Savior is now over there.

4 I'll soon be at home over there,
   For the end of my journey I see;
   Many dear to my heart, over there,
   Are watching and waiting for me.

REF—Over there, over there,
   I'll soon be at home over there.

## No. 196. Beulah Land.

1 I've reached the land of corn and wine,
   And all its riches freely mine,
   Here shines undimmed one blissful day,
   For all my night has passed away.

CHO.—O Beulah Land, sweet Beulah Land,
   As on thy highest mount I stand,
   I look away across the sea,
   Where mansions are prepared for me,
   And view the shining glory shore,
   My heaven, my home, forever more!

2 My Savior comes and walks with me,
   And sweet communion here have we;
   He gently leads me by His hand,
   For this is heaven's border-land.

3 A sweet perfume upon the breeze,
   Is borne from ever-vernal trees:
   And flowers that never fading grow
   Where streams of life forever flow.

## No. 197. Nettleton.

1 Come, Thou Fount of every blessing,
   Tune my heart to sing Thy grace;
   Streams of mercy, never ceasing,
   Call for songs of loudest praise.
   Teach me some melodious sonnet,
   Sung by flaming tongues above;
   Praise the mount—I'm fixed upon it—
   Mount of Thy redeeming love!

2 Here I'll raise mine Ebenezer:
   Hither by Thy help I'm come;
   And I hope, by Thy good pleasure,
   Safely to arrive at home.
   Jesus sought me when a stranger,
   Wandering from the fold of God:
   He, to rescue me from danger,
   Interposed His precious blood.

3 Oh, to grace how great a debtor
   Daily I'm constrained to be!
   Let Thy goodness, like a fetter,
   Bind my wandering heart to Thee:
   Prone to wander, Lord, I feel it,
   Prone to leave the God I love;
   Here's my heart, oh, take and seal it;
   Seal it for Thy courts above.

## No. 198. Oh, for a Heart.

1 Oh, for a heart to praise my God,
   A heart from sin set free!
   A heart that always feels Thy blood,
   So freely spilt for me!

2 A heart resigned, submissive, meek,
   My great Redeemer's throne;
   Where only Christ is heard to speak;
   Where Jesus reigns alone.

3 Oh, for a lowly, contrite heart,
   Believing, true, and clean,
   Which neither life nor death can part
   From Him that dwells within!

4 A heart in every thought renewed,
   And full of love divine;
   Perfect and right, and pure and good,
   A copy, Lord, of Thine.

## No. 199. Jesus, Lover of my Soul.

1 Jesus, Lover of my soul,
    Let me to Thy bosom fly,
While the nearer waters roll,
    While the tempest still is high!
Hide me, O my Savior, hide,
    Till the storm of life is past;
Safe into the haven guide,
    Oh, receive my soul at last!

2 Other refuge have I none;
    Hangs my helpless soul on Thee:
Leave, oh, leave me not alone,
    Still support and comfort me:
All my trust on Thee is stayed,
    All my help from Thee I bring;
Cover my defenseless head
    With the shadow of Thy wing!

3 Thou, O Christ, art all I want;
    More than all in Thee I find;
Raise the fallen, cheer the faint,
    Heal the sick, and lead the blind.
Just and holy is Thy name,
    I am all unrighteousness:
False and full of sin I am,
    Thou art full of truth and grace.

## No. 200.        Guide Me.

1 Guide me, O Thou great Jehovah,
    Pilgrim through this barren land,
I am weak, but Thou art mighty;
    Hold me with Thy powerful hand,
        Bread of heaven,
    Feed me till I want no more.

2 Open now the crystal fountain,
    Whence the healing waters flow;
Let the fiery, cloudy pillar,
    Lead me all my journey through:
        Strong Deliverer,
    Be Thou still my strength and shield.

3 When I tread the verge of Jordan,
    Bid my anxious fears subside;
Bear me through the swelling current;
    Land me safe on Canaan's side;
        Songs of praises
    I will ever give to Thee.

## No. 201. What hast Thou Done for Me?

1 I gave my life for thee,
    My precious blood I shed
That thou mightst ransomed be,
    And quickened from the dead.
‖: I gave. I gave my life for thee,
    What hast thou given for me?:‖

2 My Father's house of light,
    My glory-circled throne
I left, for earthly night,
    For wand'rings sad and lone.
‖: I left, I left it all for thee,
    Hast thou left aught for me?:‖

3 I suffered much for thee,
    More than thy tongue can tell,
Of bitterest agony,
    To rescue thee from hell;
‖: I've borne, I've borne it all for thee,
    What hast thou borne for me?:‖

4 And I have brought to thee,
    Down from my home above,
Salvation full and free,
    My pardon and my love:
‖: I bring, I bring rich gifts to thee,
    What hast thou brought to me?:‖

## No. 202. Bringing in the Sheaves

1 Sowing in the morning, sowing seeds of
        kindness,                    [eves:
    Sowing in the noon-tide, and the dewy
Waiting for the harvest, and the time of
    ' reaping,                    [sheaves.
    We shall come rejoicing, bringing in the

Cho —‖: Bringing in the sheaves,:‖
    We shall come rejoicing, bringing in the
        sheaves.

2 Sowing in the sunshine, sowing in the
        shadows,                    [ing breeze;
    Fearing neither clouds nor winter's chill-
By and by the harvest, and the labor ended,
    We shall come rejoicing, bringing in the
        sheaves.

3 Go, then, ever weeping, sowing for the
        Master,                    [grieves;
    Though the loss sustained our spirit often
When our weeping's over He will bid us
        welcome,                    [sheaves.
    We shall come rejoicing, bringing in the

# ✧ INDEX. ✧

[THE END.]